Cambridge Elements ≡

Elements in Music since 1945
edited by
Mervyn Cooke
University of Nottingham

FILM MUSIC IN CONCERT

The Pioneering Role of the Boston Pops Orchestra

Emilio Audissino
Linnaeus University

CAMBRIDGE
UNIVERSITY PRESS

CAMBRIDGE
UNIVERSITY PRESS

University Printing House, Cambridge CB2 8BS, United Kingdom

One Liberty Plaza, 20th Floor, New York, NY 10006, USA

477 Williamstown Road, Port Melbourne, VIC 3207, Australia

314–321, 3rd Floor, Plot 3, Splendor Forum, Jasola District Centre,
New Delhi – 110025, India

103 Penang Road, #05–06/07, Visioncrest Commercial, Singapore 238467

Cambridge University Press is part of the University of Cambridge.

It furthers the University's mission by disseminating knowledge in the pursuit of education, learning, and research at the highest international levels of excellence.

www.cambridge.org
Information on this title: www.cambridge.org/9781009009096
DOI: 10.1017/9781009006941

First published 2021

A catalogue record for this publication is available from the British Library.

ISBN 978-1-009-00909-6 Paperback
ISSN 2632-7791 (online)
ISSN 2632-7783 (print)

Film Music in Concert

The Pioneering Role of the Boston Pops Orchestra

Elements in Music since 1945

DOI: 10.1017/9781009006941
First published online: November 2021

Emilio Audissino
Linnaeus University
Author for correspondence: Emilio Audissino, emilio.audissino@lnu.se

Abstract: The Boston Pops Orchestra was the first orchestra of its kind in the USA: founded in 1885 from the ranks of the Boston Symphony Orchestra, its remit was to offer concerts of light symphonic music. Over the years, and in particular during the fifty-year tenure of its most famous conductor, Arthur Fiedler, the Pops established itself as the premier US orchestra, specialising in bridging the fields of 'art music' and 'popular music'. When the Hollywood composer John Williams was assigned the conductorship of the orchestra in 1980, he energetically advocated for the inclusion of film-music repertoire, changing Fiedler's approach significantly. This Element offers a historical survey of the pioneering agency that the Boston Pops had under Williams's tenure in the legitimisation of film music as a viable repertoire for concert programmes. The case study is complemented with more general discussions on the aesthetic of film music in concert.

Keywords: film-music concerts, Boston Pops Orchestra, Conductor John Williams, Cine-concerts, prejudices against film music

ISBNs: 9781009009096 (PB), 9781009006941 (OC)
ISSNs: 2632-7791 (online), 2632-7783 (print)

Contents

I consider movie music as a legitimate art form like a symphony or an opera.

John Williams (Ponick 2004)

1 Introduction

The past twenty years have witnessed a remarkably increased presence of film-music selections in concert programmes, not only in film-themed shows. More and more, film music has been sharing the stage with overtures and suites from the 'classical' repertoire. For example, the 2019 Summer Night Concert at the Schönbrunn Castle of the Wiener Philharmoniker saw Gustavo Dudamel conducting a selection that, alongside Gershwin's *Rhapsody in Blue*, Johann Strauss Jr.'s *Jubilee Waltz*, Barber's *Adagio for Strings*, and Dvořák's *Symphony No. 9*, also included the suite from *Casablanca* (1942, dir. Michael Curtiz) by Max Steiner, a composer who epitomises the Hollywood music, for better or for worse. The programme strongly leaned towards American music – Bernstein's *Overture to Candide* was also included – and hence the inclusion of Hollywood music can be explained by Hollywood cinema's global fame as one of America's major cultural exports. Yet, up to a few years ago, Steiner's music used to be singled out as the example of how Hollywood's Golden Age music – if not film music at large – was too fragmentary, formless, derivative, and image-dependent, with its 'tendency to provide hyperexplicit moment-by-moment musical illustration' (Gorbman 1987: 87), to be able to sustain a life beyond the films. Today, even Steiner's film music has made it to the Wiener Philharmoniker.

If the presence of the film-music repertoire in concert programmes can be said to have exploded, the academic studies of the phenomenon are lagging behind by comparison. The probable reason is that it already took a substantially long time for academics and music critics to take film music seriously enough as a type of applied music *within* the film. Many of the first studies of film music stressed the long neglect that this type of music had to suffer, referring to film music as 'a neglected art', 'unheard melodies', 'the invisible art', and to the necessity of 'settling the score'. Then, it is not surprising that accepting film music also *beyond the film* as a legitimate repertoire for concert presentations should require an extra amount of effort and time. With the increased presence of film music in concert programmes having helped supersede past prejudices, in recent years the debate has refocussed on the aesthetic legitimacy of detaching film music from its visual counterpart. Given that visuals are a fundamental formal blueprint, can film music function as stand-alone music, or does its close relation with the film require that music and images stay together for a full appreciation? One might cite the words of conductor Leonard Slatkin: 'The question always comes up: "Do you need visuals when you are listening to film music?" Let me ask you: "Do you need visuals when you are listening to opera?" My answer to both questions is no: if the music is good, it can stand by itself' (Page 2003). To which, however, one might respond with the words of the film composer and concert conductor, Elmer Bernstein: 'The music may be able to stand up very nicely outside of the film, but it's the combination that makes a great experience – the combination of music and film' (Karlin & Wright 2004: 472).

Academics have problematised the music/image separation. For example, Ben Winters states: 'By advocating the separation of the musical object from its accompanying sensory stimuli, we ignore this complex interaction and risk losing an essential part of the film score' (Winters 2007a: 116). One solution to the problem has been advanced in the form of the new modality of 'cinematic listening' (Long 2008: 7–8). It consists in the listeners envisioning some visual accompaniment to a music piece, be it one that is randomly evoked in the listener who is not familiar with the parent film or one that calls up in the mind the atmospheres and visuals of the well-known film. Frank Lehman, in particular, has studied 'film music as concert music' from this perspective:

> Avid listeners of soundtracks know well how one's frame of mind may shift upon hearing tracks from a rousing score on a personal audio device. The heightened effects and dramatic associations embedded within the average film cue have a tendency to map onto – and mythify – a cinematic listener's subjective reality in a most pleasing fashion. ...Cinematic listening is a 'process of simultaneous audiation and envisioning', and ... cinematic music is anything which 'compels the listener to engage in acts of "envisioning" some accompanying diegesis or . . . series of images.' (Lehman 2018: 11)[1]

Besides the application of cinematic listening to these traditional without-the -film formats of presentations, another solution to the problem is that of presenting film music *with* the film it was created for. This phenomenon has been called 'cine-concert' (McCorkle Okazaki 2020) or, in a previous study of mine, 'multimedia film' (Audissino 2014b: 51). An orchestra plays a film score live as the film is projected, which is a way to recover the music/visual synchronisation specific to film music.

The live in-presence performative element of the orchestra playing the musical score, added to the pre-recorded dialogue/sound and image tracks, engenders 'a sense of connection that watching the same movie at home on a streaming service cannot. Live music is a crucial ingredient in creating a communal atmosphere' (McCorkle Okazaki 2020: 7). Another advantage of multimedia film is that the music is highlighted, not only because the live

---

[1] 'Audiation' is the mental hearing and processing of sound: Gordon 1985.

performance of the orchestra inevitably brings closer attention to the musical element but also because such live performances often showcase a more detailed rendition of the music itself. This aspect is stressed by Keith Lockhart, one of the most active conductors of multimedia films and the current leader of the Boston Pops Orchestra: 'In the tracks on the old movies the orchestra is so muddy and it is so hard to hear it. When you look at the score of *The Wizard of Oz*, for instance, the orchestration is ingenious, but you could never tell that from listening to the low-res sound of the old soundtrack' (Audissino & Lehman 2018: 403). Finally – and perhaps the principal reason for their success – multimedia films are very profitable for orchestras and allow them to lure into the concert halls segments of audience that would have never attended a 'normal' concert: in Jon Burlingame's formulation, 'After years of looking down their collective noses at film music as unworthy of performance alongside, say, Beethoven or Wagner, orchestras from the Chicago Symphony to the New York Philharmonic are jumping on the bandwagon, playing classic film scores "live to picture" in growing numbers' (Burlingame 2015). Today, we see a skyrocketing increment of the number for these events: 'As of July of 2019, at least ninety films have been concertized for live performance, with the greatest number yet (eighteen) premiering in 2017' (McCorkle Okazaki 2020: 9).

In this study I argue that a pivotal and highly influential agent of change for the legitimisation of 'film music as concert music' (Lehman 2018), as well as for the development of today's multimedia films, was John Williams's tenure as the conductor of the Boston Pops Orchestra. Archival research into the history of Williams's Pops years reveals the seminal impact that his appointment to the position and his policies and experimentations throughout his tenure had on the wider acceptance of film music as concert-programme material. I have published some of my findings in previous essays (Audissino 2012, 2014a, 2014b, 2016). Here, I reinterpret and expand on my past archival work because the Williams/Boston Pops importance for the acceptance of film music as concert music has not, in my opinion, been stressed enough. For example, as regards the aforementioned phenomenon of live-accompanied films, McCorkle Okazaki's essay offers a thorough examination, but, oddly enough, her survey completely neglects to mention the Williams/Boston Pops case as an antecedent.

Before delving into how the Boston Pops Orchestra was an essential stepping stone in the concert legitimisation of the film-music repertoire, it is necessary to provide a general background of the life of film music beyond the films, along with a mention of the prejudices that have long accompanied this type of applied music and, as a consequence, have considerably contributed to the prevention of its concert presentation until recently. Some might be already familiar with the condensed survey I am about to offer, as well as with the sketch of the principal aesthetic/philosophical reasons behind the bias against film music. Nevertheless, I am convinced that providing a general backdrop for the less specialised reader is a necessary preliminary step to fully appreciate the ground-breaking nature of the John Williams/Boston Pops collaboration. An aesthetic prejudice influenced by the Romantic aesthetics has still been circulating, more or less overtly and more or less consciously, in most of the criticisms against the film-music repertoire. Even if its centrality and influence have arguably abated during the twentieth century, I am convinced that its shadow has still been exerting a sizeable role in the shaping of mindsets and axiology.

2 Film Music and Aesthetic Prejudice

Primarily, the reasons behind the prejudice against film music can be found in the aesthetics of the nineteenth century, in which an axiological classification gained currency that assigned different degrees of musical value and aesthetic weight to 'programme music' or 'applied music', on the one hand, and to *Absolute Musik*, on the other.[2] Applied music was based on some extramusical programme and created to serve some practical/functional purpose, as an accompaniment to some extramusical event or music based and shaped on some extrinsic structure – dance, theatre, a lyrical text, singing, and so on. *Absolute Musik* was composed independently from extramusical restrictions or references: 'Thereafter there is no longer a *single* concept of music, as previous generations knew it, but *two*, about whose rank and historical priority one soon begins to quarrel' (Dahlhaus 1991: 7–8). The two typologies would extend, under different formulations and names, into the twentieth century – the dichotomy between *Gebrauchsmusik* ('music for use', written for some extramusical usage) and *Vortragsmusik* ('music for listen-ing', written for the sole or primary scope of being listened to) in the 1920s mittel-Europe (Hinton 2001), or the more recent and still lingering distinction between 'art music' and 'popular music' or 'experimental music' and 'commercial music', for example. Behind the nineteenth-century term *Absolute Musik* was the philo-sophical paradigm of Idealism: 'Music was considered to be an expression of the "essence" of things, as opposed to the language of concepts that cleaved to mere "appearances"' (Dahlhaus 1991: 10). Just as absolute philosophy was 'a philoso-phy of the "absolute," interpreted or denounced as severed from its roots in earthly and human matters, and thus "absolute"' (21), and also *ab soluta* in the Latin sense ('freed from'), so the highest expression of music was the one that was similarly 'freed from' the mundane: a direct expression of the Being and the Absolute. For Wackenroder – one of the founders of the German Romanticism –

---

[2] I further discussed the Romantic prejudice against film music in Audissino 2014a.

absolute music was 'in itself already religion' (75). The consideration of musical fruition as akin to a sacred experience produced a change in the contexts and attitudes of the listening situation: music could not be any more merely a pleasant background for conversations and games of cards, as it often had been up to the eighteenth century; music should be experienced in a solemn state of quasi-religious contemplation (80). These aesthetic positions, naturally, exerted some authority on compositional practice. In his treatise *The Beautiful in Music*, Eduard Hanslick intimated that only music without a text, a function, a programme was true music: 'The composer must not allow his hands to be tied by anything alien to his material, since he ... aims at giving an objective existence to his (musical) ideal, and at casting it into a pure form' (Hanslick 1891: 100–1). For Hanslick, 'tonally moving forms are the sole content and object of music' (quoted in Dahlhaus 1991: 109). Besides this formalism – the centrality of pure musical form – organicism was another hallmark of nineteenth-century music (Meyer 1996: 190). In a piece of music, each element had to be justified by its own intrinsic, 'natural' organic development, like a tree naturally developing from a seed, growing spontaneously and inevitably, independent of external conditions and impositions (193).

From this Romantic perspective, film music is certainly not 'ab soluta': its very existence is predicated on the previous existence of a film. If for Hanslick, 'Every melody or theme has its own laws of construction and development which to the true musical genius are sacred and inviolable, and which he dare not infringe in deference to the words' (Hanslick 1891: 63–4), film composers are then sacrilegious in how they 'violate and infringe' the laws of construction and development of music to bend them to the cinematic demands. For the Romantic aesthetics, film music possesses no organicism either: its elements are not motivated by intrinsic musical necessities but by the extrinsic demands of the film. True, examples exist of film music that can fulfil the film's demands while at the same time developing into a stand-alone musical organism – instances can be found in the film music of many of the major film composers, and the organicistic compositional approach of John Williams has been called 'teleological genesis' (Schneller 2014). Yet, on the other hand, the often frag-mentary nature of film scores (one perfunctory ten-second cue, then one unre-lated twenty-three-second cue, another few seconds of music to accompany an isolated action, and so on) or the very technique of 'Mickey-Mousing' (music that closely mirrors the visual actions and hence whose development is exter-nally driven in a rigid and highly prescribed way) all tend to look like the opposite of the unbridled organicistic flow envisioned by the Romantics. Moreover, to the Romantic eye, film music is formulaic and inclined to linguis-tic borrowing from other musical works. The Romantic aesthetic found clichés and conventionality hardly acceptable. In the words of Chevalier Louis de

Jaucourt, 'The man of genius is cramped by rules and laws of taste. He breaks them so that he can fly upwards to the sublime . . .. He is constantly thwarted in his desire to express the passions that excite him, by grammar and conventions' (Meyer 1996: 172). The film composer, then, is seen as a mere artisan rather than an artist: 'The nonutilitarian pleasure of art confirms the distinction between art and craft (which almost by definition has a purpose), and it also confirms, as it were, the childlike innocence of the creative artist, for, eschewing the worldly temptations of patronage, fame, and fortune, the artist plays the game of art for its own sake' (189). It is no coincidence that the well-remunerated practical purpose of film composition has been one of the strongest arguments employed in the critics' circles to denigrate a priori the artistic validity of film music and the venal motivations of its composers. Film music apparently complies with none of the Romantic criteria for aesthetically worthy music, and though the single criterion can be contested – for example, film music can indeed have an organicistic development, as previously pointed out – it is the general labelling attitude of the Romantic aesthetics that has caused long-term effects. The assessment is not made on the individual piece of music and its merit, but there is a pre-judgement (prejudice) based on whether a type of music belongs to one category or another – applied/absolute – and the music is liable to be labelled and judged without even being actually listened to.

The Romantic aspect of nonutilitarian art versus commodified crafts was somewhat reprised by the Frankfurt School in its critical theory of the 'Culture Industry', whose products are instrumental to anaesthetise the conscience of the consumers by entertaining them, thus maintaining the ideological status quo of the ruling class. The Hollywood 'Dream Factory' was deemed to be one of the most insidious branches of such Culture Industry, and hence its film music was considered the worst form of commodified music. Hollywood Cinema and its music were vehemently criticised along these lines by Theodor W. Adorno and Hanns Eisler in their 1947 book *Composing for the Films*: 'The motion picture cannot be understood in isolation, as a specific form of art; it is understandable only as the most characteristic medium of contemporary cultural industry' (Adorno & Eisler 2007: xxxv). Within, Romantic-ideology residues are evident, for example, in the usage of 'form and content' and 'inspiration': 'The rule of big business has fettered the freedom of artistic creation, which is the prerequisite for a fruitful interaction between form and content' (42). As to film music, they state: 'All music in the motion picture is under the sign of utility, rather than lyric expressiveness. Aside from the fact that lyric-poetic inspiration cannot be expected of the composer for the cinema, this kind of inspiration would contradict the embellishing and subordinate function that industrial practice still enforces on the composer' (4). According to this view, film music is the product of a mercenary inclination and cannot be taken seriously as art: 'The truth is that no serious composer writes for the motion pictures for any other reason than money ' (37). This 'for-money's-not-for-art's-sake' argument has been systematically adopted to denigrate film music and its practitioners. For example, Stravinsky famously quipped: 'The only function of film music is to make its composer earn good money' (quoted in Calabretto 2010: 48).

These Romantic prejudices have found a remarkable diffusion in particular in those countries in which philosophical Idealism was strongly established. One such country is Italy, where the influence of Benedetto Croce's aesthetics has been central, and Italy is an interesting example of how the aforementioned a priori labelling has hindered the legitimisation of film music. From the viewpoint of Croce's Idealism, film music is not the artistic result of a free 'aesthetic intuition' but the product of hired craftsmanship, and as such, it belongs more to the 'economic dimension' of the Spirit rather than to the 'aesthetic dimension' (Croce 2005). It is no surprise that the Italian art-music composer Ildebrando Pizzetti, after agreeing to compose the score for the silent-film epic *Cabiria* (1914, dir. Giovanni Pastrone), felt awfully guilty: 'A cowardly action ..., pages and pages of meaningless music, more or less unpleasant noise, music of which I would be the first to laugh at, that would make me sick if it were composed by someone else, music beneath myself' (Miceli 1982: 78). In more recent times, at the end of the 1970s, another art-music composer, Goffredo Petrassi, rehashed the old 'for-money's-not-art's-sake' argument when he dismissed his sporadic involvement with film music as 'out of sheer economic necessity, without the slightest illusion of producing something aesthetically worthy' (Miceli 2009: 341). In addition, the academically trained composer – and Petrassi's pupil – Ennio Morricone also showed an ambivalent attitude towards his work in cinema: 'I did not approach film music by vocation: I thought I would be one of the many composers who *earn little money* [emphasis mine] but write what they want. ... I regret not doing in my life what I would have liked' (Miceli 1982: 309–10, 321) – note again the money-versus-art argument implied in Morricone's statement. Crocian restraints can be found even in some of Italy's pioneers of the study of film music. Ermanno Comuzio, on the one hand, was amongst the first to defend the dignity of film music as an object of study: 'Sometimes [musicologists] do discuss the topic, but always from a position of aristocratic disdain. ... They consider film music as a mercenary practice of little noble nature' (Comuzio 1980: 9). Having said so, when it comes to the concert presentation of film music, Comuzio takes a more conservative stance:

the practice is questionable, since these works for their very nature should not be separated from the related films.... While every other type of music (a symphony, a song, an opera) can be found both on paper and in live concerts and theatre performances or recorded on discs, film music exists only when it is played through the loudspeakers of a film theatre while the film is projected. (Comuzio 1980: 41, 117)

In 1999, Sergio Miceli, on the occasion of a radio broadcast of a BBC Proms film-music programme, commented on this largely documented Italian disdain for film-music concerts:

Considering the influence that Croce's aesthetics has had on musicology – an idea of pure music, untouched and untouchable – it is clear that applied music [tends to be seen as a minor production]. This also happens with film music, which – I always repeat it a bit polemically – is not the only type of applied music. However, it is the one that gives more trouble because there is some sort of basic misunderstanding, a basic refusal.... Film music concerts are very frequent abroad. Only here there is this negative perception of the phenomenon. (Miceli 1999)[3]

For example, until late in his career, Morricone was reluctant to perform film music in concert, and in 1979 he stated: 'Very often film music is really banal, it should not be performed. I'd be offended myself. I was invited all over the world to perform my music in concerts, and I have always declined because I perfectly knew that they wanted me to present my easiest pieces' (Miceli 1982: 313). The first noteworthy attempts at the inclusion of film-music pieces in concert programmes took place in Italy only in the 1980s (Corbella 2016), ten years later than in the United Kingdom, for example, where the 'FilmHarmonic' concerts were established in 1970.

The Italian context, for its radicalisation of the Idealist aesthetics, functions as a clear illustration of the concrete effects that this Romantic conception of music had on the delay of the concert presence of film music. If for the Romantic-influenced, Wackenroderian aesthetics music is akin to religion and listening to a concert is like attending some solemn rite, it is clear that such 'non-religious' music as film music – the least absolute of all – cannot find a place in the concert halls, the temples devoted to the contemplation of *Absolute Musik*. In the United Kingdom, to name a different context, film composition has been more accepted within the art-music circles as one of the musical outputs of the 'English Musical Renaissance' (Mazey 2020: 2), and film-music concerts found an increasingly steady place in concert halls, for example, with the already mentioned 'FilmHarmonic' series at the Royal Albert Hall. Yet, the Romantic aesthetic

---

[3] Rai Radio 3 interview of Sergio Miceli, 15 August 1999 (my translation).

resurfaced against the music hailing from Hollywood, in which 'specialists' were mostly employed. The British composer Anthony Hopkins vehemently attacked the legitimacy of Hollywood composers with a wording that betrays the Romantic 'money-versus-art' discrimination: 'Who are these people, whose names never seem to appear on any concert programmes? What else have they written; what pages have they placed upon the altar of Art rather than on the lap of Mammon?' (Wierzbicki, Platte, & Roust 2012: 141). As to the American 'Pragmatist' context, it is, oddly enough, closer to Italy, not so much because of an influence from Idealism but presumably for a combined influence of the Critical Theory of the Culture Industry (and specifically, Adorno and Eisler's book) and for the widely reported vituperative opinions that art composers who had tried their hand at cinema expressed, in frustration, against film scoring. Hollywood's strict industrial routines left less leeway and freedom to art composers than the more 'light-weight' British film industry, by comparison. Some of the harshest prejudices against film music in the USA were ignited and propagated by a trio of art musicians dissatisfied with their film experiences, George Antheil, Oscar Levant, and Virgil Thomson (Wierzbicki 2009: 2), but also Aaron Copland, Igor Stravinsky, and Arnold Schönberg contributed to variable degree to the disparaging of Hollywood's music (Cooke 2010: 257–360). Speaking of the American context, Jack Sullivan offers this summary:

> The classical intelligentsia once openly ridiculed film composing, using it as an instant metaphor for anything shallow or sentimental and scoffing at concert composers who wrote for the movies on the side.... Current critics tend to be more accepting of the field, but they practice a curious doublethink, one that is often unconscious. 'Sounds like movie music' is still a common way to dismiss a new concert work, even among reviewers ostensibly friendly to the genre. (Sullivan 2007)

If the presence of film music beyond the screens has long been ignored or deprecated in critic and academic circles – and its legitimacy (mostly) accepted only in recent times – film music as a stand-alone entity has long been consumed and enjoyed by the layperson.

3 Film Music: from the Screens to the Concert Stages

Frank Lehman thus summarises the stand-alone existence of film music:

> The list of extra-filmic musical traces is extensive and includes artefacts (sheet music, soundtrack albums), activities (performances, covers, remixes), venues (concert halls, recitals, theme parks) and discursive communities (Internet forums, enthusiast magazines, scholarship).... It is safe to say, in 2018, that more people have become familiar with the themes from *Chariots*

of Fire, *The Magnificent Seven* or *Psycho* through various extra-filmic media than have seen the movies they originate from. (Lehman 2018: 7)

Considering the entirety of film history, the main manifestations of the external life of film music can be grouped into three types: piano reductions for home performance, disc records, and adaptations for concert performance. The third incarnation – concert presentation – has been the tardiest to appear and get established, perhaps precisely because of the 'sacred' image of the concert halls as the temples reserved to *Absolute Musik* that the Romantic aesthetics had consolidated. Film-music records sold on the market as a commodity are not a 'sacrilegious' crossover: film music *is* commercial *Gebrauchsmusik*, so it is normal that it should be sold for a profit. Film-music pieces performed in concert, on the other hand, constitute a much less acceptable trespass into the realm of *Vortragsmusik*. The fact that stand-alone incarnations of film music have long existed as sheet music or records and only much later, and timidly, have started to appear on concert stages seems to suggest a different point: the crux of the matter does not lie so much in the supposedly intrinsic incapacity of film music to stand on its own as in the 'cultural-guardian' attitude instigated by the Romantic aesthetic. Film music broke the borders of the screen very soon in its history, having a life beyond the films it was composed for; what took longer was to erode the entry barriers that guarded the concert halls from 'ill-reputed' types of music.

Chronologically, piano reductions were the first form of adaptation and extra-filmic life. At the end of the nineteenth century, almost simultaneously with the birth and spread of the cinema, a veritable 'piano craze' was spreading throughout the USA (Altman 2004: 51). The vast diffusion of pianos caused the rapid and massive development of music publishing, the main output being popular songs, the so-called Tin Pan Alley music, largely sold in the form of sheet music, 'one of the nation's fastest-growing commodities . . . propelling popular tunes to a level of cultural importance that would rarely be equaled' (Altman 2004: 51). The expanding music market seized the opportunity to associate with cinema in order to promote new songs by exploiting its popularity, for example, in the form of 'illustrated song', a sort of primitive karaoke that was a fixture of the 1910s nickelodeons and was directly supported by music publishers (Altman 2004: 182–90). When illustrated songs went out of fad, the music publishing industry took advantage of the new trend of original/custom-compiled film scores by using them to exploit tie-in products. One of the earliest American examples of an originally composed/compiled film score, *The Birth of a Nation* (1915, dir. David W. Griffith), is also one of the earliest examples of this commercial exploitation. The film's love theme composed by Joseph Carl

Breil was quickly adapted by Chappell music publishing into 'The Perfect Song': it sold 10,000 copies in 1916 alone (Altman 2004: 293–4).

In the 1910s, the market was already shifting from piano and sheet music to phonographs and discs (Altman 2004: 191) and, with further technical improvements in the 1920s and 1930s, sheet music for home performance became of secondary importance, though piano reductions of popular melodies from the silver screen have continued to hold a considerable share of the market to the present day. Hollywood studios expanded their interests to the record industry too, one of the first cases being Warner Bros. taking over a record company in 1930 (Smith 1998: 33). The revenues from music records came almost exclusively from songs rather than symphonic pieces, which was also due to the limited capacity of the 78 rpm disc, accommodating four/five minutes per side, ideal for songs but not for lengthier instrumental selections. An example of film-song disc, considered the very first film-music disc release, is the 1938 issue of *Snow White and the Seven Dwarfs* (1937, dir. David Hand, music by Frank Churchill, Leigh Harline, and Paul J. Smith), which sold 1,500,000 copies (Marmorstein 1997: 278).

Symphonic scores could find some extra-filmic space in radio broadcasts, in the form of suites – Franz Waxman's *Rebecca* aired on the Pacific Coast Network on 9 May 1940 (Neumeyer & Platte 2011: 81) – or as an accompaniment to adapted radio dramas, often with the original film cast – Erich Wolfgang Korngold's *The Adventures of Robin Hood* was featured on KECA and the National Broadcasting Company (NBC) Blue Network on 11 May 1938 (Winters 2007b: 94). Yet, as regards symphonic film music – meant as orchestral music with no singing – the titles released on 78 rpm discs were decidedly fewer than film-song discs, and the early attempts made by David O. Selznick to market symphonic film music proved unsuccessful (Barnett 2010). Exceptions included *The Jungle Book* (1942, dir. Zoltan Korda, music by Miklós Rózsa), which can be considered the first symphonic film-music album (Karlin 1994: 186), and the *Warsaw Concerto* from *Dangerous Moonlight* (1942, dir. Brian Desmond Hurst) composed by Richard Addinsell (Cooke 2008: 426). Selections from *Captain from Castile* (1947, dir. Henry King) by Alfred Newman were marketed only in 1952, and Max Steiner's *Gone with the Wind* saw an album release in 1954 (RCA Victor LPM – 3227) and reached the No. 10 position in Billboard's 'Best-Selling Popular Albums' (Anon. 1954: 26).

The 1950s was a more conducive decade, in which the record industry had a spectacular expansion fuelled by the advent of the $33^{1/3}$ LPs (Smith 1998: 24–68). LPs expanded the capacity of the previous 78 rpm to circa twenty-five minutes per side, thus offering more opportunities for orchestral music, since the longer duration could give the room required for suites and medleys from symphonic film scores. The albums from *Lawrence of Arabia* (1962, dir. David Lean, music by Maurice Jarre) and *Cleopatra* (1963, dir. Joseph L. Mankiewicz, music by Alex North) were early examples of symphonic film music that met with successful LP releases (Smith 1998: 36–7).

Arguably, it was the diffusion of LP albums of film music that favoured the presentation of film-music concerts, specifically thanks to the film-music anthology albums that sprouted in the 1960s, such as those conducted by Henry Mancini (*The Concert Sound of Henry Mancini*, 1964), Elmer Bernstein (*Movie and TV Themes*, 1962), Stanley Black (*Film Spectacular,* 1962), or Muir Mathieson (who recorded a symphonic suite from *Gone with the Wind* in 1961), to name a few. Alfred Newman, one of the fathers of Hollywood music and a proficient conductor, had recorded 78 rpm discs of opera selections in the 1940s (no film music) and, after the aforementioned *Captain of Castile* album, profited from the technological innovation to release in 1953 an LP of concert versions from his own film scores on the A-side (*Wuthering Heights, Song of Bernadette, All About Eve* coupled with Gershwin's *An American in Paris* on the B-side, and this was followed by *Alfred Newman, Dean of Motion Picture Music, Conducts Themes!* (1962). In 1966, the Composers and Lyricists Guild of America sponsored an anthology album titled *Music from Hollywood*, the subtitle reading 'An In-person Recording Featuring Hollywood's Greatest Composers Conducting Their Own Works'. Arguably, the first widespread introduction of film music to the world of concert music took place during the recording sessions for these anthology albums. In such cases, the orchestra was not assembled to play music that would be mixed and fused into a film's soundtrack; the orchestra was assembled to play music intended to have an extra-filmic life as a stand-alone musical experience. Unlike the tie-in records of a given film – the so-called 'original soundtracks' – these anthologies were not primarily designed to use film music as an advertisement for a specific film but rather to present film music as music.

The 1960s anthology-album trend reached new heights in the 1970s. In particular, the 1972 LP album *The Sea Hawk. The Classic Film Scores of Erich Wolfgang Korngold* can be said to have opened a new phase. The record was released by RCA Victor and the music was played by London's National Philharmonic Orchestra under Charles Gerhardt's baton.[4] This was probably the first appearance of film music in an album that was published within a catalogue of classical music – rather than pop music – and whose conductor was not an insider with a self-interest in this repertoire but someone without personal

---

[4] On Gerhardt, see also Benson 1999.

involvement in the film industry.[5] The RCA Victor 'Red Seal' series specialised in classical-music albums – among the artists featured were Leopold Stokowski and Arturo Toscanini as well as Arthur Fiedler and the Boston Pops, interestingly enough for this survey. Gerhardt was a producer and conductor for RCA Victor, responsible for the recording of symphonic albums which we might place in the 'middlebrow' category. These albums were 'cross-over' projects aimed at popularising 'highbrow' culture within audiences accustomed to more 'lowbrow' fare, if these categories have to be adopted at all.[6] For example, in 1964, Gerhardt released with the Royal Philharmonic Orchestra an album anthology of Johann Christian Bach, Vivaldi, and Haydn, and in the following years, anthology albums such as *Elizabethan Serenade* (1976, including music by Elgar, Walton, Britten, and Arnold) and *The French Touch* (1978, featuring works by Ravel, Satie, and Fauré). Throughout the 1970s, Gerhardt seamlessly moved from the 'proper' concert repertoire to film music, recording music from both repertoires under the RCA 'Red Seal' banner. In particular, the 1972 Korngold album ushered in a long series of other anthologies, the *Classic Film Score Series*, culminating in the 1979 recording of the entire Korngold score for *Kings Row* (1942, dir. Sam Wood).[7]

Gerhardt's recordings did not try to make film music sound 'pop' – like some Stanley Black or Henry Mancini 'easy-listening' arrangements of film themes – but instead sought to maintain the original symphonic style, reconstructing from the archival sources and expanding the score from the smaller studio-orchestra instrumentation to that of a full symphony orchestra. Nor did he seek to select the pieces by a film-popularity criterion, but from a musical stand-alone one: 'I determined to re-create these scores or selections from them in the original orchestrations . . ... When selecting the contents I was always concerned with the quality of the music, not with that of the film. Times without number great music has been written for average films' (Karlin 1994: 230). The 'Classical Film Score Series' has been acknowledged to have had the fundamental function of

---

[5] It must be said, though, that George Korngold – Erich Wolfgang's son – was the producer of this first album.

[6] On highbrow and lowbrow, see Levine 1988.

[7] Gerhardt's film-music RCA Victor albums were *Now Voyager: The Classic Film Scores of Max Steiner* (1973); *Classic Film Scores for Bette Davis* (1973); *Captain from Castile: The Classic Film Scores of Alfred Newman* (1973); *Elizabeth and Essex: The Classic Film Scores of Erich Wolfgang Korngold* (1973); *Casablanca: Classic Film Scores for Humphrey Bogart* (1974); *Gone with the Wind: The Classic Film Scores of Max Steiner* (1974); *Citizen Kane: The Classic Film Scores of Bernard Herrmann* (1974); *Sunset Boulevard: The Classic Film Scores of Franz Waxman* (1974); *Spellbound: The Classic Film Scores of Miklós Rózsa* (1975); *Captain Blood: Classic Film Scores for Errol Flynn* (1975); *Lost Horizon: The Classic Film Scores of Dimitri Tiomkin* (1976); *Star Wars and Close Encounters of the Third Kind* (1978); *The Spectacular World of Classic Film Scores* (1978); *Music from the John Williams Score Star Wars Return of the Jedi* (1983).

introducing the classical Hollywood repertoire to a wide audience (Wierzbicki 2009: 202). One of its effects was one of legitimisation, showing that if film music could appear within the 'Red Seal' classical-music series, then it could also start appearing in concert programmes. Moreover, Gerhardt's recordings also required the preliminary edition of the performance materials (score and parts), and afterwards said materials could be made available to other orchestras as well, facilitating further performances. It is no coincidence that the company 'Themes and Variations', specialising in the rental of film-music performance materials, was founded in 1977, right in the midst of Gerhardt's 'Classical Film Score Series' decade.

In the USA there were few film-music concerts before the 1970s. The film-music concert that took place on 25 September 1963 at the Hollywood Bowl was reported as an exceptional event (Kendall 1992). Prior to the 60s, attempts had been made, but reviews were mixed and the reception unpredictable. In 1943 Max Steiner had conducted the New York Philharmonic at Lewisohn Stadium in a programme of his own and Alfred Newman's and Victor Young's music, and reviews were harshly dismissive (Smith 2020: 297–9). In the same year, Eugene Ormandy presented a suite from Bernard Herrmann's *The Devil and Daniel Webster* in a Philadelphia Orchestra programme, and reviews were much warmer and positive (Smith 2002: 101).[8] Sources emphasise Elmer Bernstein's commitment to popularising film music in the 1960s (Hasan 2004: 30; Miceli 2009: 236), and the fact that Mancini was the first Hollywood composer to tour nationwide conducting film-music concerts (Marmorstein 1997: 332) seems to confirm that before that decade there was little room and acceptance for film music in concert programmes.

What type of concert programmes, though? Jeff Smith points out that the albums of orchestral film music are purchased by the same people who would buy anthologies of the classics or of light symphonic music. Both types of albums cater to an audience that appreciates instrumental music and the many colours and nuances of a symphony orchestra but is dissatisfied with the esoteric and impenetrable works produced by contemporary art-music composers:

> a substantial block of light classical music lovers, who appreciated the film score's emphasis on hummable melodies and tasteful arrangements. With classical music patrons increasingly alienated by the adventurous new works of Milton Babbitt, Pierre Boulez, and John Cage, record executives might

---

[8] The sharp contrast in the critical response to Steiner's and Herrmann's concert suites could also be read as a product of the labelling that aesthetic prejudices attached to music: the music by the cinema/operetta composer Steiner from Hollywood, one of the industry's most prolific employees, was dismissed; the music by the freelance composer/conductor Herrmann from New York, and collaborator of the 'artsy' Orson Welles, was praised. Tellingly, Herrmann, the less Hollywood-y of US film composers, was the first one to receive academic attention in the 1970s, and has been nicknamed the 'Beethoven of Film Music' (Rosar 2003).

well have hoped that scores by Rózsa, Newman, and North would sell alongside the works of Strauss, Wagner, and Tchaikovsky that inspired them. (Smith 1998: 49)

What Smith notes about the record industry can be applied to live concerts too. In the Darmstadt School-inspired 1960s, 'absolute composers' would stay clear of tonality and write music that sounded even meaningless to most people.[9] Examining the 1960s high-culture context, Leonard B. Meyer stated: 'Experimental music is often a set of relationships to be studied, not music to be heard. It is not, like language, a means of communication but, like mathematics, an object of investigation' (Meyer 1967: 278). For those with a preference for more communicative tonal music, there were few new entries played in 'serious' concert programmes, with the staples still consisting of the usual pre-twentieth-century canonical works – the 'classics'. Cinema was thus one of the few steady sources of new tonal symphonic music capable of communicating to the masses: 'The world of film scores is the popular interface with the world of orchestras', as admitted by the conductor Keith Lockhart (Audissino & Lehman 2018: 402). The live-concert equivalent of those anthology albums in which film music found one of its first and successful outlets were anthology concerts programming selections from the 'best of' of the classical canon as well as pieces of light symphonic music. If attending a concert whose programme is entirely occupied by a Mahler or a Bruckner symphony is like committing to a demanding – and to some, indigestible – formal dinner, light symphonic concerts are like enjoying a more casual drink with tapas.

Light symphonic programmes are made of varied and typically short (less attention-demanding) selections of operatic overtures, suites from ballets, symphonic marches, and excerpts from famous symphonies. In Europe, the most noted instances are the 'Promenade Concerts', most notably the BBC Proms in London: a summer concert series given by the UK's major orchestras at the Royal Albert Hall, which also include popular programmes at affordable prices and in a more casual setting. Other instances are the New Year's concert and the summer concert at the castle of Schönbrunn by the Wiener Philharmoniker, or the summer concerts of the Berliner Philharmoniker at the Waldbühne, for example, the 'Russian Night' (20 June 1993, Seiji Ozawa conductor), whose anthology programme included: *Russian Easter* Overture (Rimsky-Korsakov); Suite from *The Nutcracker* (Tchaikovsky); *Polovtsian Dances* (Borodin); Suite from *The Firebird* (Stravinsky); *1812 Overture* (Tchaikovsky); *The Sabre*

---

[9] The comprehension and appreciation of a music style surely depends on the degree of musical education and familiarity with said specific style (Meyer 1956: 35, 160). However, some scholars also maintain that the tonal system is more natural than atonality and hence of more universal appeal (Meyer 1956: 76, 1996: 322; Sloboda 1999: 197, 235, 257).

Dance (Khachaturian); Elegia from *Serenade for Strings* (Tchaikovsky); *Radetzky March* (Johann Strauss I); *Berliner Luft* (Paul Lincke). Like in the anthology albums, the programme is organised around an overarching theme (Russian music), and the pieces are famous 'warhorses' of an easy-listening nature, with popular additions like the beloved *Radetzky March* or *Berliner Luft* that cater to the mittel-European audience. In America, these types of programmes are traditionally offered by 'Pops Orchestras'. The oldest, and the point of reference for all the other subsequent US Pops orchestras, is the Boston Pops. On its centennial, in 1985, David Tomatz, director of the Moores School of Music at the University of Houston, celebrated the orchestra's importance in these terms: 'The influence of the Boston Pops is quite astonishing . . . . By performing popular music so wonderfully, by setting such a high standard, they've set a standard for the entire industry' (Wood 1985). During the orchestra's centennial celebration, at the helm of the orchestra was the Hollywood composer John Williams, and from that prestigious podium he would advocate for a better consideration of the film-music repertoire.

4 The Boston Pops and Popular Music

Having founded, in 1881, the Boston Symphony Orchestra (America's second oldest after the New York Philharmonic and one of the historic 'Big Five'[10]), in 1885 Henry Lee Higginson – Boston resident, businessman, and philanthropist – also established a series of light-music concerts to be held between spring and summer in the city's Music Hall. The first, pressing reason was to provide the Boston Symphony members with employment also in the musically vacant summer season. The second reason was to import in the USA the entertaining and casual atmosphere of the Viennese open-air concerts which Higginson had attended and much appreciated when in Europe:

> Concerts of a lighter kind of music, in which should be included good dance music . . . to keep the prices low always, and especially where the lighter concerts are in question . . . My judgment would be that a good orchestra would need, during the winter season, to keep its hand in by playing only the better music, and could relax in summer, playing a different kind of thing. (BSO 2000: 16).

In Higginson's statement, we find, on the one hand, the patron-of-the-arts eagerness to make music available, enjoyable, and affordable to as many people

---

[10] Gaining currency during the 1950s, the 'Big Five' ranking included the longest established, most prestigious, and financially strongest ensembles in the USA: besides the Boston Symphony, the other four were the New York Philharmonic (established in 1842), the Chicago Symphony Orchestra (established in 1891), the Philadelphia Orchestra (established in 1900), and the Cleveland Orchestra (established in 1918). The elite group has evolved and changed during the years, with new entries and exits. See Kirshnit 2006.

as possible. The bridging and even educational function of such light-music concerts – introducing the larger popular audience to symphonic concerts – resounds strongly in Higginson's words, and this philosophy would characterise the Boston Pops throughout its history. Yet, on the other hand, we can detect in the founder's words that Romantic labelling that tends to separate 'high music' from 'low music': 'better music' in the winter official symphonic season, and in the summer 'relax' with 'a different kind of thing'. This conflicting attitude would regularly resurface in the Boston Pops' history: On the one hand, the pride of reaching out to a wider audience through the presentation of popular music; on the other hand, the consideration of such popular music something inferior, if not outright demeaning for the BSO musicians.

The first 'Promenade Concert' was held on 6 May 1885 under the baton of Adolf Neuendorff.[11] An indicative sample of the first season is the 11 July concert, here transcribed from the original print programme:

> March – *Imperial* (Resch);
> Ouverture – *William Tell* (Rossini);
> Waltz – *Mon Reve* (Waldteufel);
> Selection – *Little Duke* (Lecocq);
>
> Intermission
>
> Overture *A Morning, Noon and Evening in Vienna* (Suppé);
> Reminiscences from *Tannhauser* (Wagner);
> *Pizzicato Polka* (Strauss Jr.);
> *An Evening with Bilse* (arr. Ernst Scherz);
>
> Intermission
>
> Overture – *Die Felsenmuhle* (Reissiger);
> Waltz – *Donau Lieder* (Strauss Jr.);
> Paraphrase – *Loreley* (Nesvadba);
> Galop – *Shooting Star* (Bial).[12]

The Viennese and mittel-European influence is quite noticeable: operetta excerpts, two Strauss entries, and a medley of famous excerpts from the classics repertoire dedicated to Benjamin Bilse (1816–1902), a well-known light-music composer and conductor in Berlin at that time.[13] The three-part structure of the programme should also be noted – three sections with two intermissions – which

---

[11] The name derives from the European outdoor concerts. In Boston the concerts were indoor but the 'Promenade' term might have been kept as a homage to band conductor Patrick Sarsfield Gilmore, a renowned Bostonian who had been the first to import the European outdoor concerts to the USA. See Gilmore 2010.

[12] https://archive.org/stream/bostonpopsorches1885bost/Pub_1885_POPS#page/n80/mode/1up.

[13] See www.berliner-philharmoniker.de/en/history/beginning/benjamin-bilse-and-hermann-wolff/.

would remain the trademark of the Boston Pops format until the 2010s. In 1900, 'Symphony Hall' was opened to become the Boston Symphony's new home, and the Promenade Concerts also moved there and started to be more conveniently called 'Pops'. The European influence was a strong one throughout the initial period: the first seventeen conductors were all European born. They imported not only the European catalogue of classics but often also some Romantic prejudices, which contributed to the exacerbation of the aforementioned friction between the Pops' popularising mission and the more or less veiled contempt for all things popular. One of these European conductors was the Italian composer Alfredo Casella (1883–1947), whose appointment lasted only from 1927 to 1929 because of the patrons' complaints. The 'Casella incident' is an interesting case in point. Casella misunderstood the Pops' mission, or perhaps he refused to implement it. He started to programme less and less popular music and more and more art music to such an extent that he included not excerpts but entire Beethoven symphonies (21 June 1929), presented all-Wagner programmes (10 June 1929), and even contemporary art-music compositions like Arthur Honegger's *Pacific 231* (30 April 1928), a dissonant 'machine music' piece hardly consistent with the Pops' fare. The 26 June 1929 concert is illustrative of the direction taken by the Italian conductor: Beethoven's *Symphony No. 6* in the first part; Casella's own *Concerto Romano, for Organ and Orchestra, Op. 43*, in the second; Ravel's *Daphnis et Chloé: Suite No. 2* in the third. A direct witness commented that 'Casella had upset the whole idea of the Pops by turning them into a Summer Symphony, and the audience stayed away in droves' (Humphrey 1980). After dismissing Casella, the BSO board of directors appointed the Boston-native Arthur Fiedler (1894–1979), a BSO violinist. He had built his credentials through two significant actions: during the Casella years he had founded an orchestra, the Boston Sinfonietta, and offered his own alternative light-music concert season. Moreover, he had launched the free outdoor 'Esplanade Concerts' on 4 July 1929, which has remained an Independence Day tradition in Boston ever since.[14] Fiedler explained: 'You can get great literature free at your public library. Arts come free at museums. Why can't you get great music free of charge?' (BSO 2000: 36). He was committed to bringing music to the masses – as he would say, 'classical music for people who hate classical music' (Adler 2007). Fiedler also showed an unabashed open-mindedness for the light-music repertoire: 'There's nothing wrong with playing light music. You don't always read Milton, Shakespeare, and Schopenhauer. You can enjoy Mark Twain' (BSO 2000: 37). During his multi-decennial tenure – from 1930 to his death in 1979 – he reinvented and shaped the Boston Pops into what they are now: an American

---

[14] The 'Esplanade' is a large open space near the Charles River in Boston on which the Edward A. Hatch Memorial Shell is placed, a covered hemispheric concert stage projecting onto a spacious lawn.

institution – 'America's Orchestra' – and one of the most widely known orchestras in the world as a consequence of its extensive presence on television, radio,
and the record market. Originally, the orchestra was known as 'the orchestra of
the pops concerts' and was mostly a local institution. In 1935 Fiedler signed
a contract with RCA Victor and ushered the orchestra into a long series of
successful album releases: for that occasion the orchestra was christened
'Boston Pops Orchestra'. Fiedler's Boston Pops albums would sell a total of
around fifty million copies over the decades (Dyer 1985: 12). He also pioneered
the media expansion, launching local live radio broadcasts in 1952, which were
expanded to reach a national diffusion in 1962. In 1967 the Pops moved to
television, and from 1969 to 2004, they had their regular nationally aired TV
programme, *Evening at Pops* – with circa 250 episodes in almost forty years, it
made the Pops the only orchestra in the world with such media exposure (Dyer
1982).[15] Fiedler's 'Fourth of July' 1976 Esplanade Concert – celebrating the
bicentennial of the Declaration of Independence – was telecast nationwide and
had a live-audience attendance of more than 400,000 people, setting the record for
the largest audience for a symphonic concert at the time (BSO 2000: 13).

As for concert programmes, Fiedler retouched them both in terms of form and
in terms of content. He further institutionalised the traditional three-part programme and assigned, as in a well-balanced menu, precise musical characters,
and 'nutritional factors' to each section:

> It struck me that this general public was snobbish about what they called
> 'classical' music, and the 'classical-minded' crowd was snobbish about music
> which they called 'popular' with an air of condescension. Accordingly, I laid out
> programs in three sections planned so as to provide something of interest for the
> greatest variety of tastes in the course of an evening. . . .. Usually the first part [of
> the program] has some good music in it, the middle part is a soloist, and the last
> part is gumdrops – which people like and which I think are perfectly all right and
> I have no shame about it. (BSO 2000: 36)

As in Higginson's case, we can see in Fiedler's words an open-mindedness
and a willingness to bridge the musical gap between the highbrow and the
lowbrow – the Boston Pops is precisely acknowledged as an example of
middlebrow culture.[16] According to *Washington Post*'s music critic Joseph

---

[15] Produced by Boston's WGBH Television and by the Boston Symphony, the series was broadcast
nationwide by PBS (Public Broadcasting Service), always ranking in the top positions of the
network's viewing figures (Jennes 1980: 48). On the history of *Evening at Pops* see Bachman
1989 and Rich 2000.

[16] For example, in Ayden Adler's paper 'The Critical Response to Profitable Concerts: Arthur Fielder
and the Boston Pops Orchestra, 1930 – 1950', delivered at the 'Music and the Middlebrow
International Conference', 22–24 June, London: www.musicandthemiddlebrow.org/conference/pro
gram/. The middlebrow as an aesthetic category has also a research network: www.middlebrow-
network.com/About.aspx.

McLellan, the strategy worked: 'Those long-ago concerts were not all fluff;
Liszt, Brahms, Beethoven and Rossini made regular appearances. A classical
concerto would usually occupy part of the evening. The little goodies usually
came at the end, and while we were patiently waiting for dessert, we were given
some very substantial music. Many of us developed a taste for the serious stuff'
(McLellan 1985). Yet, on the other hand, we can still perceive some residues of
the old categories both in Fiedler's wording ('good music' the classical repertoire, and 'gumdrops' the popular) and in McLellan's ('fluff' and 'goodies'
versus 'substantial' and 'serious' music). In concrete, however, Fiedler contributed to the smoothing of these once-hard borders and rankings by programming
the two repertoires together. If the first part of the programme was reserved for
the classics of the symphonic repertoire, it was in the second and third part –
respectively showcasing a soloist from either the classical or the popular arena
and featuring the popular repertoire – that Fiedler introduced considerable
programming changes. As the first American-born conductor, he expanded
the repertoire to include more American music: 'So I started with Gershwin
and with show music and television music and radio music. Most of the
orchestra players were French and when we started playing this music, they
mostly looked down they noses at it' (BSO 2000: 36). Modifying the preference
of his European predecessors for the European repertoire of concert music,
Fiedler started to introduce what, compared to the venerable Canon, could be
considered popular *Gebrauchsmusik*: marches, show tunes, Tin-Pan Alley
songs, jazz-influenced music, the products of the young and mass-oriented
American culture. Besides presenting the then brand new compositions of
Gershwin and adding more pieces of America's 'March King' John Philip
Sousa – whose *The Stars and Stripes Forever* soon became the Pops' musical
signature – Fiedler also commissioned new pieces from compatriot
composers.[17] A favourite was Leroy Anderson (1908–1975), who had been
Fiedler's chief arranger since 1936 and expressly composed for the Pops a series
of amusing and inventive symphonic miniatures as *The Typewriter, Sleigh Ride,
Jazz Pizzicato*, and *Fiddle-Faddle*, which have since become staples of the light
symphonic repertoire. In the third part of the programmes, Fiedler opened the
door of symphonic concerts to the Broadway musical repertoire – which would
increasingly take the place of the old selections from operettas – and to jazz:
such artists as Ella Fitzgerald, Dizzy Gillespie, Benny Goodman, and Lionel
Hampton performed on the Symphony Hall stage during the Fiedler years. In
the final two decades of his tenure, Fiedler also ventured into the field of

---

[17] *The Stars and Stripes Forever* (1896) has long used to be played at the end of each Boston Pops
concert. The première of the symphony-orchestra version of Sousa's march had been given by
the Boston Pops on 2 July 1897 (BSO 2000: 48).

youngsters' pop music and featured in the third part orchestral arrangements of the Beatles' current songs and of disco-music hits too.

Fiedler's success was also financial and soon became an indispensable asset for the BSO Inc.: in the Fiedler years, the income from the Pops Season, lasting two months, was one-third of the annual total revenue – the Symphony season lasted seven months (Goodson 1980). His policy of programming the classics side by side with popular music and the financial success – the 'commodification' of music – caused clashes with the 'cultural guardians' of art music. *Boston Globe*'s Richard Dyer reports an exemplifying comment from Fiedler's first decade:

> Naturally, not everyone approved. 'Since when has it become necessary for the Boston Symphony Orchestra, which is rated as one of the best in the world', wrote a suburban resident in a letter to the editor of the *Boston Herald*, 'to stoop to jazz in order to draw an audience out of the city reputed to be the center of culture? Mr. Fiedler is showing remarkably poor judgment and taste by including such numbers as "Strike Up the Band."' (Dyer 1985: 11)

An emblematic case was the tense relationship between Fiedler and Boston Symphony's Music Director Serge Koussevitzsky (1874–1951), Russian-born and carrying from Europe the usual baggage of Romantic prejudices. Koussevitzsky notoriously despised the Pops. Reportedly, he would complain that 'when the orchestra arrived at Tanglewood to begin the summer festival [after the Pops season], . . . they "sounded like the Pops" and [he] worked to put them back into "shape"' (Speyer 1984). On one occasion Koussevitzsky, 'rudely "disinvited" Fiedler from conducting a BSO concert because he had seen Fiedler's name on a Symphony Hall poster announcing a Frank Sinatra concert' (Dyer 1985: 12).

When Fiedler passed away at eighty-four on 10 July 1979, the BSO management had to face a daunting task: to find a successor to the legendary figure that Arthur Fiedler had become. At that point, the conductor of the Boston Pops had become a celebrity and a point of reference for other orchestras all over the country. As stated by Richard Dyer, 'the music director of the Boston Pops automatically becomes one of the most famous musicians in the world, and one of the most sought-after as a guest' (Dyer 1980a). In Boston, the search for the new Pops conductor was accompanied by 'the media ballyhoo usually reserved for presidential candidates' (Pfeifer 1980a) and was compared to the task of 'choosing a new Pope' (Swan et al. 1980: 85), but the appointment process – described as 'feverish as the dragnet for Scarlett O'Hara' (Jennes 1980: 48) – also gained a nationwide coverage. A 'Committee on the Future of the Pops' had been formed as early as April 1979 (Pfeifer 1980a), when Fiedler was already seriously ailing, with the scope of taking care of the task of finding a successor. Besides BSO board members, trustees, executives, the General Manager Thomas W. Morris, and Music Director Seiji Ozawa, it also included three external members: the producer of the television show *Evening at Pops* William Cosel, the rock promoter Don Law, and Luise Vosgerchian – chairperson of the Harvard music faculty (Pfeifer 1980a). The committee had already undertaken a laborious selection process by asking the members of the orchestra to rate each guest conductor with expressly designed questionnaires, 'rating a conductor excellent, good, fair or failure in approximately a dozen categories. They were asked how clear a conductor's beat was, whether he was pleasant to work with, whether they would like him invited back, whether they would like him as a permanent conductor' (Pfeifer 1980a). Besides the questionnaires, a key person-specification was the high musical profile that the candidate was expected to possess, as reportedly pointed out by Harvard's Professor Vosgerchian: 'She kept in mind the feeling of the orchestra musicians who "want to maintain a certain artistic level" at Pops, who "want to feel clean when they come out of a Pops concert." . . . "What makes it difficult," she said, is that "playing music which is vogue can be either delightful or agonizing"' (Pfeifer 1980a).

As soon as Fiedler passed away, the committee speeded the process up, and in October a shortlist was prepared, ranking the finalists according to their score in the evaluation questionnaires: John Covelli, Erich Kunzel, Mitch Miller, Harry Ellis Dickson, and John Williams (Dyer 1980b). While the other candidates were either popular-music public figures, like Miller, or more experienced conductors, like Covelli and Kunzel, Williams had an exiguous concert-conducting track record at the time, having worked principally as a studio conductor for his own music. He had just barely begun to be invited to publicly conduct his film works in concerts after the vast success of *Star Wars* (1977, dir. George Lucas) and its all-symphonic score, which was soon adapted into a thirty-minute suite and premiered by Zubin Mehta and the Los Angeles Philharmonic in 1977 (Swed 2012). Coincidentally, Williams had also acted as a last-minute replacement for an incapacitated Fiedler at one Hollywood Bowl concert in 1978 (Burlingame 2000: 20), and in May 1979 he was invited to guest-conduct the Boston Pops. Yet, BSO's violinist Sheldon Rotenberg revealed that during those guest-conducting appearances, Williams 'received more "excellents" than any of the others' in the evaluations cards (Pfeifer 1980a). In December, when the committee was asked to accelerate and select a favourite, Williams jumped to the top position – he also received the endorsement of André Previn and Leonard Slatkin (Dyer 2002 and Score Masters: Celebrating John Williams and Jerry Goldsmith: 01.21.25). Observers speculated that such choice could have been a result of the Pops willing to take part in the recording of some of his film scores, a very profitable extra-job already undertaken by some orchestras, like the London Symphony for *Star Wars* – 'a chance to capitalize, literally, on their new conductor and his film work' (Goodson 1980).[18] Others pointed out the two essential advantages that Williams had over others: 'skills as a music arranger' (Miller 1980) and the fact that 'he could bring excellent television and recording opportunities' (Pfeifer 1980b). Harvard's Professor Vosgerchian explained, 'What attracts me most about Williams is his arranging and composing skills. . . . No matter what is in vogue on the Pops scene, he could give it a certain class' (Pfeifer 1980c). Introducing better standards for the Pops repertoire was crucial because the quality and tastefulness of the arrangements of the popular material had been a sour point in the final years of Fiedler's tenure, as we shall see. Moreover, there was an element of kinship between Williams and Fiedler: What the latter had done as a conductor, the former had achieved with *Star Wars* and his other film scores, which 'exposed the general movie audience to the symphonic sound. In this way, he is similar to Fiedler, whose televised performances with the Boston Pops brought symphonic sound to the TV masses' (Goodson 1980).[19]

An analysis of the two programmes that Williams guest-conducted in 1979 is indicative as to why Williams had shown to be up to the job – see Figure 1.

Williams's second 26 May concert differed in its replacement of Anderson's *Irish Suite* with Mozart's *Horn Concerto no. 2 in E Flat*. These two programmes were in harmony with Fiedler's tradition, yet they offered interesting innovations. The first part featured British music represented by selections that were less known but still palatable for the general audience – Vaughan Williams and Walton – and not as hackneyed as the usual staples of the Pops 'classical classics', like the *Barber of Seville* overture. Indeed, Williams would expand the 'classics' repertoire with a number of entries from the British concert

---

[18] In the end, the Boston Pops could never be booked to record any film score. Attempts had been made with the Luciano Pavarotti vehicle *Yes, Giorgio* (1982, dir. Franklin J. Schaffner), which had a sequence filmed at Boston's Hatch Shell; with *E.T. The Extraterrestrial* (1982, dir. Steven Spielberg) and later with *The Witches of Eastwick* (1987, dir. George Miller), all cancelled because of schedule conflicts (Dyer 1981, 1988). Only minor contributions were possible: the additional music for the 1980 director's cut edition of Spielberg's *Close Encounters of the Third Kind* (1977) and the diegetic chorus for the Thuggee human sacrifice in *Indiana Jones and the Temple of Doom* (1984, dir. Steven Spielberg) were both recorded in Symphony Hall with the Pops (McKinnon 1983). After Williams's tenure, the Itzhak Perlman parts of the score for *Schindler's List* (1993, dir. Steven Spielberg) were recorded in Symphony Hall with members of the Boston Symphony. At last, the entire score for *Saving Private Ryan* (1998, dir. Steven Spielberg) was recorded in Symphony Hall with the Boston Symphony and the Tanglewood Festival Chorus.

[19] On how John Williams revived symphonism and the 'classical Hollywood style' in the 1970s cinema through his 'neoclassical' scores, see Audissino 2021.

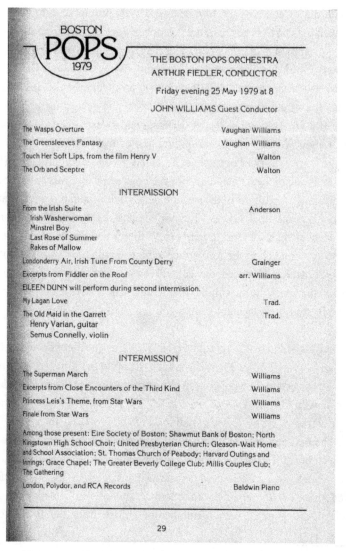

Figure 1 25 May 1979 programme, guest conductor John Williams
(Courtesy BSO Archives, used by permission)

music – 'serious' contemporary music and yet accessible enough – starting with Michael Tippett's *Suite for the Birthday of Prince Charles* during his first season as Pops' appointed conductor (5 May 1980). Moreover, one of the items was a film-music piece, William Walton's *Henry V*, and the significant placement of such film-music piece in the first part of the programme, usually reserved for the art-music classics, was already a foretaste of Williams's future policy about the film-music repertoire. In the central part of the 25 May programme, Williams fittingly paid tribute to Leroy Anderson and the Boston Pops tradition with the *Irish Suite*, while in the 26 May alternate programme, he showcased his handling of a revered item from the classical Canon, Mozart's *Horn Concerto*. Then he presented a Broadway piece (*Fiddler on the Roof*) in his own Academy Award-winning 1972 arrangement for violin and orchestra, complying with the custom according to which the second part of the programme should feature a soloist. This *Fiddler on the Roof* entry was also instrumental in showcasing Williams's talent as an arranger – the Pops already had another version of *Fiddler on the Roof* (arranged by Jack Mason). By listening to the two, it is striking how Mason's follows the rules of easy-listening music and is melody-driven, more static, homophonic, and musically uniform. Williams's, on the other hand, has a more symphonic design, featuring call-and-response exchanges between the orchestra's sections, polyphonic and contrapuntal writing, like a more musically challenging mini concerto for violin and orchestra, including concertante violin cadenzas.[20] On the one hand, we have music from the popular repertoire treated as pop material; on the other hand, the same is treated as symphonic-concert material. This is what Harvard's Professor Vosgerchian arguably meant with 'a certain class' as regards Williams's arrangements: he followed a symphonic conduct, not the style of Broadway show tunes or easy-listening pop, and hence his arrangements were more befitting for a symphonic institution like the Boston Pops/Boston Symphony. In the third part, traditionally including straight popular music, Williams presented his own film output and demonstrated that it possessed a stand-alone quality, was technically challenging enough for the orchestra musicians, and yet had popular appeal for the Pops' audience. BSO General Manager Thomas Morris explained that Williams 'came here ... as the composer of "Star Wars."' but, he added, 'I went to one of his concerts, and I was impressed by what I saw and heard: there was nothing of the bandwagon approach that others were taking with his music' (Dyer 1980c) – where amongst the 'others' we can include Fiedler and the arrangement of the *Star Wars* 'Main Title' that he had presented with the Pops, as we shall see.

On 5 January 1980, the *Boston Herald* spread the rumour according to which Williams was being offered the job (Pfeifer 1980b). Commentators soon elaborated on how unlikely it was that Williams should accept the offer, given that it would have been a financial loss for him: 'What remains questionable is whether the BSO could offer Williams a sweet enough deal to devote

---

[20] Mason's arrangement can be heard in the CD *The Arthur Fiedler Legacy. From Fabulous Broadway to Hollywood's Reel Thing* (Deutsche Grammophon, 2007, 477 6124), or here: https://youtu.be/zK5czM6qE3g, accessed 27 November 2020. Williams's arrangement is featured in *That's Entertainment* (Philips Records, 1981, 416 499–2), or here: https://youtu.be/K7A8fKnfTvo, accessed 27 November 2020.

full-time to the Pops. Money would be a big consideration because Williams is at the top of his profession in the movie-music business' (Pfeifer 1980b). In what the media described as an 'intrigue plotted by Eric Ambler or John Le Carre' (Dyer 1980c), Thomas Morris secretly flew to London to meet Williams – who was there to record his score for *The Empire Strikes Back* (1980, dir. Irvin Kershner) with the London Symphony Orchestra. At 1.00 a.m. GMT on 9 January 1980, the much-awaited signature was secured: John Williams succeeded Fiedler as the nineteenth conductor of the Boston Pops. The decision was saluted positively in some more musically progressive quarters, for example, by André Previn, then conductor-in-residence of the London Symphony and a versatile musician who had worked in Hollywood, the musical theatre, jazz, and classical music, seamlessly: 'The Pops is lucky that John is available. He is a first-class pianist, and he knows a terrific amount of music. Furthermore, he knows the orchestra from the point of view of the man with the pencil, and that means intimately' (Dyer 1980a). BSO concertmaster Joseph Silverstein described Williams as 'an extremely well-schooled and sophisticated musician . . .. I know much of his serious music and it's first class' (Pfeifer 1980c). Pops' concertmaster Emanuel Borok, who would be one of the warmest supporters of Williams's appointment – 'It's like someone new, young, dynamic and exciting moving into a grand old house and redecorating it, . . . and the level of everything is much, much more sophisticated' (Knight 1980) – promptly envisioned the major issue that Williams would have to cope with: 'I would not like to be in his shoes with the tough guys in the orchestra and those in the audience who say we know you only as being from the movies' (Miller 1980). Borok was quite prescient in his statement, as Williams's background as a film composer was seen in some quarters as a stigma: Fiedler might have played popular music, but at least he came from the classical-music world; Williams came from Hollywood. Revealing a hint of distrust, the media pointed out that 'nobody was more surprised than the management of the Boston Pops to learn that Williams was seriously interested in the position in the first place. . .. Why would he even consider leaving or cutting back on his career as the most prestigious (and most highly-paid) composer of film music?' (Dyer 1983: 12). Some were 'shocked at the selection' and characterised the appointment, euphemistically, as 'a curious choice' (Pfeifer 1980c). Others from the classical-music intelligentsia voiced their outrage in unequivocally direct terms: Jordan N. Whitelaw, the producer of the TV series *Evening at Symphony* – which, opposite to *Evening at Pops*, presented 'respectable' art music – stated that 'Williams made no impression on me whatsoever. His music shouldn't happen to a dog. I don't think anyone in the orchestra could have conceived that he would have been named conductor . . . ' (Kart 1980).

Williams would be a target throughout the 1980s for the slings and arrows of classical-music critics still guided by nineteenth-century criteria of Romantic purity. For example, reviewing a concert that Williams guest conducted with the Los Angeles Philharmonic in 1983, the *Los Angeles Times* music critic sneered: 'Why would Carlo Maria Giulini, a man of lofty principles and impeccable taste, entrust a presumably serious winter-season program to John Williams, an amiable musician whose claim to fame and fortune are predicated on movie-score bombast and Boston Pops bagatelles? . . . Why would our cultural guardians want to devote an entire evening's diet to such junk food?' (Bernheimer 1983). 'Lofty principles', 'serious program', 'cultural guardians', all still betray a reverent, parareligious idea of music, on the one hand, while 'junk food', on the other, is deliberately employed to evoke the vilest form of mass-produced, and unhealthy, commodity. In 1988, we had a different reviewer but the same disdain for the popular repertoire, the performers of such repertoire, and those who enjoy it, not too implicitly dismissed as a simple-minded, if not altogether mindless, herd ('Pavlovian'):

> John Williams brought his lackluster music and conducting to Orange County. . .. As a composer, Williams knows how to manipulate cliches. . .. But away from the glamorous images, his music sounds threadbare, endlessly repetitive, overblown and heavily indebted to serious composers. . .. As a conductor, Williams is a determined student of the metronome school, using mechanical arm gestures, occasionally injecting scooping movements with both hands and apparently, when really engaged, pumping both arms alternately as if climbing a ladder. . .. The Pacific Symphony played as if it were one big characterless studio ensemble. No one, from soloist to whole orchestra, marred the placid surface with vitality, interpretation or real expression. . .. Nonetheless, many in the audience seemed to adore Williams. Little pockets of fans gave him the now-Pavlovian standing ovation. (Pasles 1988)

If not openly belittled, even in neutral or supportive coverage, Williams was recurrently presented as the 'movie composer' and the 'millionaire', still demonstrating the power that the old binary labels (art/commerce, absolute music/applied music) still exerted. Williams is 'a multimillionaire better known to mass audiences for his Hollywood movie scores' (Stewart 1984); while Fiedler was called 'a legend', the successor was identified as 'a goldmine' (Pfeifer 1980c); a personal profile in 1980, while praising his skills, still stressed out the commercial motivation of his works: 'One wonders about a conservatory-trained musician who decides to live and work in Hollywood' (Goodson 198). The money focus is a recurrent, even obsessive one: 'It is said he can make up to $150,000 a film plus a percentage of the final profits' (Dyer

1980b); 'With fees and royalties from movies such as "Star wars" and the just released "Indiana Jones and the Temple of Doom," Williams is a millionaire and the highest paid composer in music history' (Miller 1984a). Williams's wealth appears to be such a fixation that a 1983 profile was fully devoted to how much he earned, to the point of even including precise figures and an interview with his business manager: 'Williams has made more money than any film composer before him' (Wessel 1983). Granted that a fascination for the rich and successful is a trait of the public opinion at large – think of America's evergreen 'self-made man' celebratory discourse – this obsession with Williams's earnings in music-criticism articles seems to stem from those Romantic categories that we have previously considered. The Romantic artist is by nature unacknowledged and underappreciated, even a starving outcast in the stereotypical bohemian depiction or in the 'myth of the unappreciated genius' as described by Leonard Meyer:

> At once saint and seer, the genius through inspired vision reveals new worlds and, because he is 'ahead of his time', is misunderstood, neglected, and vilified.... What the myth of the suffering, sacrificing artist did was to enhance the new audience's belief in the sincerity of the composer's inspiration and in the seriousness and value of the works of art he created. (Meyer 1996: 181–2)

The 'suffering and sacrificing artist' and the 'multimillionaire movie composer' are evidently opposites: one makes either art or money, not both. Even if the Pops was supposed to be an orchestra open to the popular trends of the day, it still comprised some of the personnel and was followed by some music critics and patrons who had been educated within the Romantic paradigm. The criticism that Fiedler had received in his first decade for daring to programme Gershwin's symphonic jazz, Williams received it for being a film composer and for aiming at legitimising the film-music repertoire as a viable one for concert presentation.

5 The Boston Pops and Film Music

Contrary to the doubts of the early analysts, Williams agreed to commit to the Pops full time during the concert season, to reside in Boston, and to reduce his film-composing engagements, explaining that his acceptance of the post was 'not a career decision, nor a financial decision, although I am amply satisfied with my new arrangement .... I see this as primarily a musical decision, a chance to make music on a level I haven't had' (Downie Jr. & Jolna 1980). In the first press conferences, Williams illustrated his plans. The first objective was the renewal of the repertoire through the injection of new pieces, both in the third part of the programme and in the first part, 'possibly to broaden the range of Pops offerings in the manner of London's Proms concerts, to include more serious works than Mr. Fiedler customarily offered', said Williams (Rockwell 1980). During his tenure, Williams would renew the usual line-up of nineteenth-century opera overtures and symphonic excerpts with British additions: for example, William Walton's *Concerto for Viola* (17 May 1983) or Frederick Delius's *Brigg Fair, an English Rhapsody* (8 May 1987). He would rediscover pieces by under-represented American composers: for example, Robert Russell Bennett's *Suite of Old American Dances* (4 July 1980), Peggy Stuart Coolidge's *Pioneer Dances* (15 July 1980), George Whitefield Chadwick's 'Hobgoblin' from *Symphonic Sketches* (7 May 1980), or the first symphonic arrangement of Alfred Burt's Christmas carols (*A Christmas Greeting*, arranged by Alexander Courage, 16 December 1980). He would commission new symphonic mini-atures expressly for the Pops: for example, John Corigliano's *Promenade Overture* (10 July 1981), William Bolcom's *Ragomania: A Classical Festival Overture* (4 May 1982), Peter Maxwell Davies's *Orkney Wedding with Sunrise* (10 May 1985), Joseph Schwantner's *Freeflight* (9 May 1989), or William Kraft's *Vintage Renaissance* (10 June 1989). Williams explained:

> We need to keep putting forward the idea that within the Pops setting we have the opportunity to create new light music for orchestra. And I find as I talk to composers that they're anxious to write pieces that are fun and enjoyable. What I try to say to my colleagues in the composing community is, 'Hey, write us a brilliant piece for a Pops audience, for an audience that doesn't attend symphony concerts'. (Katz 1989)

If the refurbishment of the first and second part could be done through rediscoveries and new commissions, the third part was the most difficult area of intervention. Williams was well conscious of the challenge posed by having a high-rank symphony orchestra play popular music, as he detailed: 'The audience comes in and leaves; the orchestra plays night after night, and only a varied repertory will hold their interest and keep the energy level . . .; the state of the orchestra means a lot to me' (Dyer 1981).

To keep the orchestra interested, the third part was refurbished with more musically challenging arrangements of the popular material. The notorious issue of what many called 'trashy arrangements' (Dyer 1980d) had character-ised Fiedler's final decade. Specifically, the late conductor's guiding criterion seemed that of assigning priority to the latest musical hits, regardless of their suitability to being played in a symphonic setting, as well as privileging the easy-listening immediacy over more inventive and musically stimulating arrangements. Richard Dyer has aptly commented upon the difficulties associ-ated with the popular repertoire:

> Well into the 1950s, the Broadway stage was still the major source of popular songs, and the idiom of the stage was compatible with the sound of the symphony orchestra. But with the development of rock 'n' roll, music was moving in another direction that left a symphony orchestra with little to do. The Pops solution was not satisfactory. Until the '50s, the Pops could play current hits more or less straight.... Later arrangers were less skillful and tasteful, and their efforts to transcribe pop and rock hits for orchestra were bloated and absurd. (Dyer 1985: 13)

This had the effect of alienating most orchestra members and of heightening the prejudice that nothing good or tasteful could come from the popular repertoire. A blatant example of such 'bloated and absurd' efforts was the rock and disco-music arrangements that Fiedler commissioned in the 1970s. On 13 May 1970, Fiedler presented a rock 'n' roll version of Bach's third Brandenburg concerto performed by the New York Rock 'n' Roll Ensemble, and during the rehearsal *Evening at Pops* producer William Cosel recalls 'watching the orchestra walk off in disgust, leaving Arthur Fiedler on the stage' (Bachman 1989: 34). Another notorious example was Fiedler's version of 'A Fifth of Beethoven', a disco arrangement by Walter Murphy of the principal theme of the first movement of Beethoven's Fifth Symphony, popularised by its inclusion in the film *Saturday Night Fever* (1977, dir. John Badham). Disco arrangements of the classics were a common practice in the 1970s, an expression of disco music's 'pluralistic cultural diversity, a diversity that, at least initially, was reflected in the large variety of musical styles and approaches that were incorporated in the disco phenomenon' (McLeod 2006: 347). If the idea of turning one of the centrepieces of the 'Canon' of *Absolute Musik* into a disco-music hit might irritate the purists but still had a cultural *raison d'être*, the Pops' Richard Hayman rearrangement into a light-symphonic version was decidedly much harder to justify.[21] One thing was the provocative translation – and cultural appropriation – of Beethoven into the then-current idiom of disco music; another thing was to have a symphony orchestra that, instead of the original symphonic version, played an orchestral arrangement of a disco cover of a symphonic piece. It was difficult to see a motivation for such arrangement/rearrangement somersault other than merely pandering to the latest musical fad. Murphy/Hayman's 'A Fifth of Beethoven', regularly programmed in the 1977–1979 period, was one of those vituperated arrangements that disappeared as soon as Williams stepped in.

Williams rejected this undiscerning approach from the outset: 'There are some things that shouldn't be tried. A symphony orchestra is never going to swing the

---

[21] 'A Fifth of Beethoven' can be heard at 50.25 into the video of the 1977 Fourth of July concert, WGBH Media Library and Archives, Boston, MA. The original Walter Murphy cover can be heard here: https://youtu.be/-KspJ_T3DnM, accessed 27 November 2020.

way a jazz band does, it is never going to rock the way a rock band does. In arranging music for the Pops it is important not to ask musicians to do something they shouldn't do, and that they cannot do' (Dyer 1980e). The middlebrow quality of the Pops entails, it can be argued, a continuous effort to keep a sensible balance between the highbrow and the lowbrow, trying to make the two meet halfway in a congruous and possibly tasteful way. If Fiedler was hired to inject more lowbrow material into an orchestra that had been pushed too much in highbrow territories by his predecessor Casella, Williams's duty now was to inject more highbrow material in order to counterbalance Fiedler's excessive doses of lowbrow. As with 'classical' concert music in the first and second part of the programmes, one solution could come from the rediscovery of the past. Williams confessed, 'one thing I feel passionately about is American popular music' (Swan et al. 1980: 86) and it was in the symphonic possibilities of the 'Great American Songbook' that Williams saw a source of rediscoveries:

> Some of our greatest composers were songwriters who were not orchestrators in the way that the great classical composers were. Their work has come to us through the work of an outside orchestrator. Some of these composers were very lucky: I think of Richard Rodgers, who had Robert Russell Bennett working for him throughout most of his career. . ... But most of our songwriters were not as lucky as that, and most of their work is in very poor shape. Gershwin is in pretty good shape, because Ferde Grofé was around, but most of the work of his contemporaries is in unspeakable condition. In the period between the First World War and about 1950 there was an explosion of creativity, but there are no definitive orchestral versions of the work of Porter, of Irving Berlin, of Harold Arlen, a major writer, of Harry Warren, of Jimmy McHugh, of Jerome Kern, who may have been the greatest of them all. One of the things I would like to see done for future generations not only of Americans but of everyone would be to have this treasure of ours put into shape for orchestra. (Dyer 1980e)

Williams, from the very first season, enlisted the services of some of the most accomplished orchestrators and arrangers, including Alexander Courage, Angela Morley, Morton Stevens, Sid Ramin, Jonathan Tunick, and Herbert Spencer, to name some, people who were all familiar with popular and film music but who could also translate it proficiently into the symphonic treatments suitable for the Pops. Williams's pursuit of a balanced middlebrow consisted precisely in selecting those items in the popular repertoire that were idiomatically suitable for a symphony orchestra, presenting them in the form of musically interesting arrangements, and performing them with artistic commitment. He elaborated on the notion in these terms:

> Popular music played by a symphony orchestra doesn't have to be trashy. It can be done in a stellar way. When I was in Europe last winter I heard

a concert by the Vienna Philharmonic conducted by Lorin Maazel, a concert of Strauss waltzes and other light things. The musicians were smiling and having a good time, but there was also seriousness in their faces as they played with felicity, subtlety, and perfection of ensemble. There isn't an English word to express that attitude of combining seriousness and fun, though there may be one in German, but that's what I think the Pops should be. And that's what I'll strive for – everyone having a wonderful time and making an exemplary musical presentation. (Livingstone 1980: 76)

Fiedler was surely open enough to accept the popular repertoire. Yet, in his mindset some residues could still be identified of the old 'art music' versus 'popular music' axiological divide. Think of the condescending qualification of 'gumdrops' for the pieces in the third part of the programmes, where the popular music would be confined, as if in a ghetto, or Fiedler's habit of sacrificing musical form in order to indiscriminately programme whatever was popular at the moment. Williams's approach was one that sought to elide these ossified categories to treat all types of music with equal respect and artistic commitment. In one of the new conductor's first profiles, *Boston Herald*'s Ellen Pfeifer already noted that Williams 'approaches classical and popular music alike with the same respect, adventurousness and love' (Pfeifer 1980d), while Pops' Associate Conductor Harry Ellis Dickson would later admit: 'I've learned a good deal from him. He taught me to value music that I would have looked down upon. He once said that a tune by Jerome Kern can be as beautiful in its way as a song by Schubert. And he is right' (Pfeifer 1993).

In his inaugural Boston programme as the newly appointed conductor (29 April 1980), televised in the PBS series *Evening at Pops*, Williams already implemented some of his renovation plans – see Figure 2. Opening the concert was a film-music piece, an overture from *The Cowboys* (1972, dir. Mark Rydell) expressly adapted by Williams from his own film score. On the one hand, Williams, the composer/conductor introduced himself as such, opening his first concert with one of his own works. On the other hand, the placement of a film overture specifically designed for concert presentation in the leading position of the prestigious first part of the programme aimed to prove that the film-music repertoire could provide musically solid pieces standing on their own in concerts. The world-renowned violinist Isaac Stern joined the orchestra to play a piece from the art-music repertoire.[22] The second part began with a film-music classic, Walton's *Prelude and Fugue* from *The First of the Few* (1942, dir. Leslie Howard), and continued with a world première: Williams's

---

[22] Williams and Stern had previously collaborated on the film version of *Fiddler on the Roof* (1971, dir. Norman Jewison), of which Williams was the music arranger and Stern the soloist.

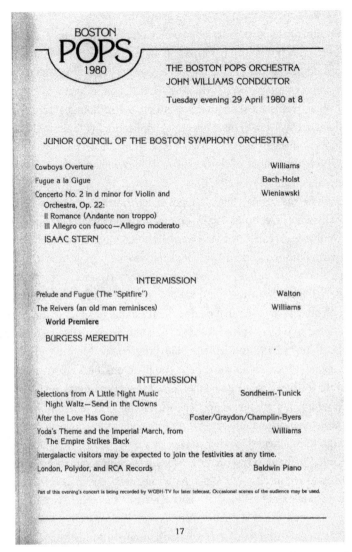

Figure 2 John Williams's Boston debut as newly appointed Pops conductor, 29 April 1980 (Courtesy BSO Archives, used by permission)

concert suite for narrator and orchestra from his own score for *The Reivers* (1969, dir. Mark Rydell), with Burgess Meredith reciting the narrator's parts.[23] The third part featured selections from Broadway, the symphonic version of a recent pop song, and two musical previews of the upcoming film *The Empire*

---

[23] Meredith was another connection Williams had made in the film industry, as Meredith served as the narrator in the 1969 film too.

Strikes Back. A special treat closed the show: the robots C3-PO and R2-D2 of *Star Wars* fame made a surprise appearance on the Symphony Hall stage, and C3-PO borrowed Williams's baton to conduct the *Star Wars* 'Main Title', with R2-D2 providing cadenzas in the form of electronic beeps.[24] From this very first concert, commentators noted Williams's equal commitment to all types of music: 'What seems most impressive is that his scrupulous care for details and stylistic purity seem to have universal application' (Pfeifer 1980d), as well as the higher musical quality: 'Two tunes from "A Little Night Music" in precise, subtle orchestrations by Jonathan Tunick replaced the Pops' previous trashy arrangements' (Dyer 1980d).

Although he had warned that 'changes in repertoire . . . can only be slow and gradual' (Downie Jr. & Jolna 1980), commenting on the preparation of his first season, Williams revealed: 'In May we will be playing more than 60 numbers in the first part of the evening, and of them approximately 35 percent are things the orchestra hasn't seen before, at least in this context' (Dyer 1980e). Much of this new material came from the film-music repertoire. If after the 1950s popular music took stylistic detours that made it increasingly unsuitable for symphonic presentations, art music too had ceased to be a largely employable source of new materials. If in the 1930s Fiedler could programme Maurice Ravel's 1928 *Bolero*, in the 1960s art music's new compositions had grown increasingly indigestible for the general audience, as we have previously discussed about the light-symphonic albums. The reservoir in which to find new material that was at the same time suitable to perform for a symphony orchestra and access-ible enough for the general audience was music written for films: 'The success of the movies Williams has scored has brought sweeping symphonic soundtrack scores back to popularity; the music he wrote, and other music by composers working in comparable styles ... could refresh the third part of the Pops programs' (Dyer 1985: 13). Williams had made it clear from the outset that he intended to make film music a substantial ingredient of his Pops programmes and 'bring prestige to the best film music by presenting it in a concert format' (Dyer 1980f). He argued:

> I suppose most film music is not very good, but most music isn't very good. What we play of the 18th and 19th century music, or even of the 20th century music, is only the best two percent, or perhaps even one percent of what was written in those years. If you culled through the music of films and took the best two percent of it, you'd probably have some very good music indeed. (Dobroski & Greene 1984: 9)

---

[24] Note at the foot of the concert programme the mention that 'Intergalactic visitors may be expected to join the festivities at any time'.

The presence of the film-music repertoire on the Pops' stage was nothing new. Fiedler too had programmed film music. As early as 1947, he presented the piece 'Orizaba' from Dimitri Tiomkin's score to *Duel in the Sun* (1946, dir. King Vidor), which was programmed nine times in the 1946/1947 and 1947/1948 seasons. Film music was, though, a rare presence, and the few attempts would be ephemeral: for example, Alfred Newman's 'Prelude' from *Captain of Castile* (1947, dir. Henry King) was premiered at the Pops on 29 May 1959, and its last appearance in the Fiedler era was a mere month later, on 20 June 1959; 'Excerpts' from Victor Young's *Around the World in 80 Days* (1956, dir. Michael Anderson) was programmed seven times across the 1957/1958 and 1959/1960 seasons. It is significant that no film music by Hollywood's foremost 'symphonist', Korngold, was ever performed by Fiedler, and that the only piece by Steiner was the theme from *A Summer Place* (1959, dir. Delmer Daves) – popularised as a pop song – and not his more symphonic-styled works. The one and only appearance of Steiner's 'Tara's Theme' from *Gone with the Wind* (1939, dir. Victor Fleming) in the Fiedler era was during a guest-conducted concert (Eric Kunzel, 10 June 1970).

An increase in the programming of film music could be observed in the 1960s, but again, significantly enough, prominent film scores in a symphonic idiom were not featured, despite the success of their films – for example, Jerome Moross's *The Big Country* (1958, dir. William Wyler), Elmer Bernstein's *The Magnificent Seven* (1960, dir. John Sturges), and Alfred Newman's *How the West Was Won* (1962, dir. John Ford, Henry Hathaway, and George Marshall) never found a place in Fiedler's programmes. Two of the most recurrent pieces from the film-music repertoire in the 1960s programmes were Henry Mancini's 'Moon River' from *Breakfast at Tiffany's* (1961, dir. Blake Edwards) and Ernest Gold's 'Theme from *Exodus*' (1960, dir. Otto Preminger). Mancini's is a theme song, and if the original version of the 'Theme from *Exodus*' is compared to Fiedler's, it is evident that the Pops' arrangement was based not so much on Gold's score as on the cover versions of the theme that had been circulating in the record market – for example, the Ferrante & Teicher 1960 easy-listening arrangement that hit no. 2 position in the 23 January 1961 'Hot 100' Billboard chart.[25] Ernest Gold's original is treated more symphonically, with inner voicing, a developmental handling of the melody, and some dissonant passages in the harmonic texture.[26] Fiedler's arrangement brings the melody and its

---

[25] www.billboard.com/charts/hot-100/1961-01-23, accessed 19 October 2020. One of the many pop/song covers, sung by Andy Williams, can be heard here: https://youtu.be/tNMetYtiUs4, accessed 5 October 2021.

[26] Ernest Gold's original theme played by the Sinfonia of London Orchestra, can be heard here: https://youtu.be/Uce14QOjlzk, accessed 5 October 2021.

hummable quality to the fore, pruning off the elements that might disturb the recognisability of the famous tune and complicate the easy-listening experience.[27]

Apart from some rare and short-lived instances in the 1950s, when Fiedler chose to programme film music, he chose it not as *film music* but as a sub-genre of the up-to-date pop genre, and he would choose the one in a pop language, assimilable to the pop-song repertoire, and with an easy-listening quality suitable for the third part of the programmes. Some of the film-music pieces programmed by Fiedler in the 1970s include 'Theme from *Love Story*' (1970, dir. Arthur Hiller, music by Francis Lai); 'The Entertainer', Scott Joplin's ragtime arranged for orchestra by Marvin Hamlisch for *The Sting* (1973, dir. George Roy Hill); 'Lara's Theme' from *Dr Zhivago* (1965, dir. David Lean, music by Maurice Jarre); 'Smile' (from *Modern Times*, 1936, dir. and music by Charles Chaplin); 'Theme from *Romeo and Juliet*' (1968, dir. Franco Zeffirelli, music by Nino Rota); 'Theme from *A Man and A Woman*' (1966, dir. Claude Lelouch, music by Francis Lai); 'Raindrops Keep Falling on my Head' (*Butch Cassidy and the Sundance Kid*, 1969, dir. George Roy Hill, music by Burt Bacharach); 'Theme from *The Way We Were*' (1973, dir. Sidney Pollack, music by Marvin Hamlisch); 'Gonna Fly Now' (from *Rocky*, 1976, dir. John G. Avildsen, music by Bill Conti); 'Staying Alive' (by the Bee Gees, from *Saturday Night Fever*, 1977, dir. John Badham); 'Theme from *Zorba the Greek*' (1964, dir. Mihalis Kakogiannis, music by Mikis Theodorakis). The fact that it was film music was of no interest per se: the interest was for its being 'pop' and a current hit. Consider the inclusion of Rota's theme from *Romeo and Juliet*: this English-flavoured modal love theme probably would not have been programmed had it not been previously adapted into a successful song titled 'What is a Youth?'[28] Fiedler favoured new pieces: the exceptions 'A Summer Place', 'Smile', and 'Theme from *Exodus*', though older, were still enjoying a market diffusion thanks to their song versions and covers. He would select those instrumental pieces with a recent successful performance in the easy-listening record charts ('Lara's Theme', 'Theme from *Love Story*', and the sirtaki from *Zorba the Greek* are such cases), or songs popularised by a film's soundtrack ('The Way We Were', or 'Raindrops Keep Falling on my Head'). He would have all these entries arranged according to a homogenous 'pop' idiom, regardless of the origin of the music – Broadway, Hollywood, top-ten charts . . . The standard Pops sound could be identified in a basically homophonic treatment that gave high prominence to the hummable melodic line; a saturated texture aimed at achieving a loud and showy presence; a pop-influenced emphasis of the

---

[27] Jack Mason's arrangement for the Pops can be heard here: https://youtu.be/4TBqGZQNV0o, accessed 5 October 2021.

[28] Lyrics by Eugene Walter: *Romeo & Juliet: Original Soundtrack Recording* (Capitol Records, 1968, ST 2993). The song is also known as 'A Time for Us' or 'Ai Giochi Addio'.

rhythm section, with drum kits added as much as possible; an opera-influenced bel canto-like writing for the violins, for the sentimental passages. Finally, the confinement of the film-music repertoire in the 'gumdrops' third part was still the rule throughout the 1970s, despite the rediscovery of the symphonic film music by Korngold and others that the Gerhardt RCA Victor albums had initiated.

Some programmes can better illustrate Fiedler's policy about film music. On 22 June 1978 (Michel Sasson, guest conductor) selections from famous sci-fi films are presented in 'electronic arrangements' for synthesisers and orchestra – in compliance with the synth pop fad of the day – and shared the third part with a medley of Beatles' hits – see Figure 3. On 14 June 1978 (Norman Leyden, guest conductor) film music, not in original versions but in pop arrangements, is once again featured in the third part, among the American standard songs – see Figure 4.

The Hollywood composer Henry Mancini, author of the 'Pink Panther Theme', guest conducted the Pops (9, 10, 11 May 1978) as well as Johnny Green, Head of the MGM music department at the time of the Arthur Freed musicals (27, 29 May 1979), and they both presented film-music excerpts. On 7 June 1977, the English composer, arranger, jazz musician, and bandleader Stanley Black (1913–2002), guest conducted and programmed a medley of his own themes from television shows, as well as Jerry Goldsmith's march from *Patton* (1970, dir. Franklin J. Schaffner) – yet, again, not in its original symphonic idiom, but in a lighter arrangement by Black. Apart from the exception of the Mancini all-film music programme, in the programmes of the film personalities Green and Black film music was still material for the third part of the programmes, and appropriately selected and arranged to fit the expected pop style of the third part. An illuminating example of the routine 'pop-isation' of all film-music items is Fiedler's version of the *Star Wars* 'Main Title'. Williams's was arguably one of the most symphonic-styled film scores since Korngold's 1930s Hollywood heydays, and a suite from the score had been presented by Zubin Mehta and the Los Angeles Philharmonic Orchestra in a sold-out concert at the Hollywood Bowl on 20 November 1977.[29] Moreover, the album was a hit, certified 'Platinum' by the Recording Industry Association of America as early as 17 August 1977.[30] In sales, popular it was. In style, it was not, according to Fiedler's 'gumdrops' standards. The 'Main Title' was presented by Fiedler

---

[29] See Cyrus Meher-Homji, 'Zubin Mehta. The Los Angeles Years', *Eloquence Classics*, 29 October 2018, www.eloquenceclassics.com/zubin-mehta-the-los-angeles-years. The program also included Gustav Holst's *The Planets* and Richard Strauss's *Thus Spoke Zarathustra*.

[30] 'Star Wars', accessed 5 October 2021, www.riaa.com/gold-platinum/?tab_active=default-award&ar=John+Williams&ti=Star+Wars+%28soundtrack%29#search_section.

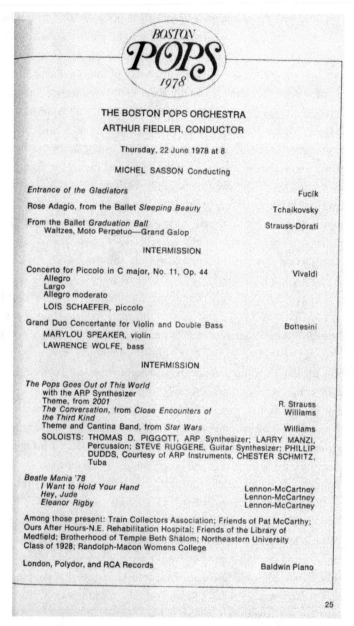

Figure 3 Michael Sasson's programme, 22 June 1978 (Courtesy BSO
Archives, used by permission)

on 6 June 1978, in the third part of the programme and in a simplified
arrangement by Newton Wayland and Richard Hayman titled 'Theme and
Dance from *Star Wars*' – see Figure 5.

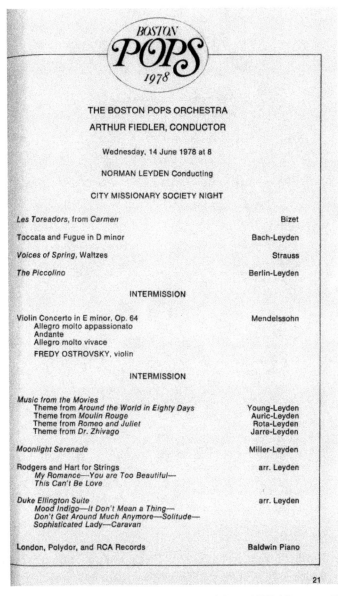

Figure 4 Norman Leyden's programme, 14 June 1978 (Courtesy BSO Archives, used by permission)

After a rewrite in which the canon-like interaction of the trumpets and trombones of the opening fanfare is removed, contrapuntal writing is flattened down, and spurious cymbal clashes are generously sprinkled all over the piece to spice it up, then Wayland and Hayman's version segues, by way of a stylistically incongruous Spanish-sounding bridge, into a Charleston-like

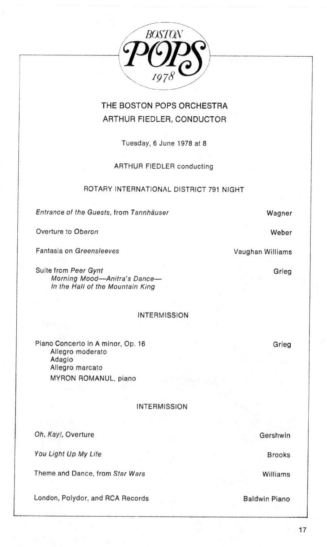

17

Figure 5 Arthur Fiedler's premiere of 'Theme and Dance from *Star Wars*',
6 June 1978 (Courtesy BSO Archives, used by permission)

arrangement of the 'Cantina Band', the diegetic music that in the film is the
backdrop of the Mos Eisley scene.[31] One generally resorts to arrangements

---

[31] 'Theme and Dance from *Star Wars*' was released for the first time in the CD *The Arthur Fiedler Legacy. From Fabulous Broadway to Hollywood's Reel Thing* (Deutsche Grammophon, 2007, 477 6124), with the deceptive title '*Star Wars*: Main Title' and without any mention of the arrangers' names, thus passing it off as the original version. It can be heard here: https://youtu.be /VkVxUdzLJjY, accessed 5 October 2021.

when the original score is either unavailable or unfitting to the ensemble supposed to play it. As for *Star Wars*, the original score was already written for full symphony orchestra and thus perfectly suitable for the Pops layout, and the score was widely available for rental – it was estimated that between 1978 and 1979 some 400 performances of the *Star Wars* suite took place around the USA (Livingstone 1980: 76). The reason for arranging the piece, consequently, seems to be that of conforming it to the Pops' trademark sound, to turn it from symphonic to 'pop' in order to be admitted into the third part of the programmes.

Upon his arrival, Williams changed the outlook on film music. The innovation lay in the search for material in the film-music repertoire that was musically interesting, not only topical and with a hit-of-the-moment appeal. Film music could fuel and enrich the symphonic repertoire, not merely the pop ranks. This was implemented by having film-music pieces featured in the first part of the programme too, traditionally reserved for the concert-music classics. On 7 May 1980, Williams opened the programme with Korngold's 'The Sea Hawk Overture' from the 1940 swashbuckler (dir. Michael Curtiz). Not only was this the first time Korngold's symphonic film music was admitted to the Pops' programmes, but it was showcased in the first part, on the same level as the operatic overtures and concert-music excerpts – see Figure 6. Other pieces of symphonic film music were placed in the first part, for example, Alfred Newman's 'Conquest' from *Captain from Castile* on 19 May 1981 and Bernard Herrmann's 'Overture' from Citizen Kane (1940, dir. Orson Well) on 10 July 1980 (in an arrangement by Ross Hastings).

If rethinking the placement of film music in the programmes without the old categories (first part versus third part) was one part of the strategy, the strongest part was the unprecedented philological care of the presentations: symphonic film music was offered in its original orchestration, not in spurious pop arrangements. Unlike previous cases like 'Theme and Dance from *Star Wars*', Williams would bring in the original versions, not only for film-music classics like Korngold's – his music from *Captain Blood* (1935, dir. Michael Curtiz) and *The Adventures of Robin Hood* (1938, dir. Michael Curtiz and William Keighley) also entered the Pops repertoire – or Jerome Moross's 'Main Theme' from *The Big Country* (on 22 May 1981). Contemporary works were also showcased as to their musical qualities, like Goldsmith's 'Closing Titles' from *Alien* (1979, dir. Ridley Scott) on 12 June 1980, the 'Main Title' from *Masada* (TV series, 1981) on 21 June 1981, and the theme from *Star Trek: The Motion Picture* (1979, dir. Robert Wise) on 7 June 1983; or Mancini's 'Penny Whistle Jig' from *The Molly McGuires* (1970, dir. Martin Ritt), a sort of miniature concerto for piccolo/penny whistle and orchestra premiered on

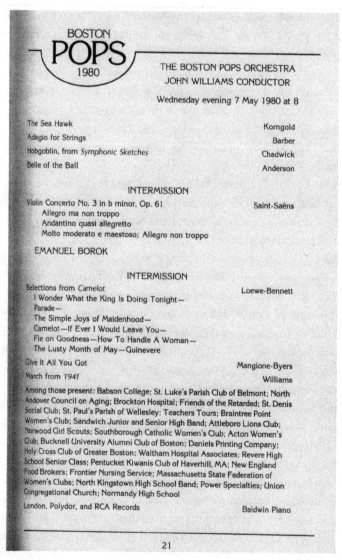

Figure 6 The overture to *The Sea Hawk* from Erich Wolfgang Korngold's 1940 film score opens the concert, 7 May 1980 (Courtesy BSO Archives, used by permission)

30 April 1985 with James Galway as a soloist. If the originals were not available, Williams would commission new arrangements based on the music as heard in the film, reconstructed from surviving orchestral parts or sketches and from the film's original music track: 'Williams likes to have older music, and current music, orchestrated in the style of its own period rather than gussied

up into an omnipresent and rootless "Pops" style' (Dyer 1983: 43). For example, Williams commissioned Alexander Courage to reconstruct Conrad Salinger's original orchestration of *Singin' in the Rain* (1952, dir. Stanley Donen and Gene Kelly), premiered on 12 May 1981. Max Steiner's 'Tara's Theme' from *Gone with the Wind* debuted at the Pops on 12 May 1982 in a faithful arrangement by Angela Morley; Dimitri Tiomkin's theme from *Friendly Persuasion* (1956, dir. William Wyler), again arranged by Morley, premiered on 19 June 1982; David Raksin's main theme from *The Bad and the Beautiful* (1952, dir. Vincente Minnelli) was added to the repertoire on 11 May 1988 in an arrangement by Herbert Spencer. Other notable film-music pieces that Williams added to the repertoire were the overture from *Lawrence of Arabia* (1960, dir. David Lean) in Maurice Jarre's own version instead of the previous Richard Hayman arrangement (23 May 1997); Elmer Bernstein's theme from *The Magnificent Seven* in an arrangement by Christopher Palmer (30 May 1989); James Horner's 'Somewhere Out There' from *An American Tail* (1986, dir. Don Bluth) in Allyn Ferguson's arrangement (5 May 1987); Horner's theme from *Glory* (1989, dir. Edward Zwick) in Alexander Courage's arrangement on 14 May 1991; Danny Elfman's suite from *Batman* (1989, dir. Tim Burton) in an arrangement by Christopher Bankey on 7 June 1994. It is interesting to note that for his 30 June 1982 concert Williams changed the name of what had been so far presented as '"Gonna Fly Now" from *Rocky*' (reading like a pop song) into 'Theme from *Rocky*' (reading like a film theme), which is indicative of a conception of film music that was evolving from a subgenre of pop music to a conception of film music as a repertoire in itself. Already in 1980, observers had noticed that Williams's attitude was more oriented to film music that was interesting as music rather than film music that was appealing as a pop hit of the moment: 'Williams has been searching out worthy film music that has been all but lost with the original motion pictures' (Pfeifer 1980d).

Unlike Casella, who attempted to modify the Pops by erasing the popular repertoire (thus arguably appeasing the orchestra members but alienating the audience) and Fiedler, who was seemingly ready to admit anything with a popular appeal (thus arguably appeasing the audience but alienating the orchestra members), Williams attempted to strike a balance by improving the musical level and presentation of the popular repertoire. He commented, 'I remember the old saying that a lot of things done in the name of art contain less art than those done in the name of commerce. I continue to try to do both, and I'm not any less serious about one or the other' (Livingstone 1980: 76). Williams's committed and serious handling of the popular material was not universally accepted in the orchestra, though, and this clash of different attitudes towards the popular repertoire brought the conductor and the orchestra to a breaking point in 1984, a crisis so central in the news coverage and in Boston's public opinion that it was dubbed 'Popsgate' (Buell 1984).

6 The Popsgate of '84

At the end of 1982, Williams's two-year contract was renewed as an 'open-ended contract' (Pfeifer 1982). Once again, newspapers voiced their surprise about the 'millionaire movie composer' willing to continue to devote his time to concerts: 'the sheer pleasure Williams appears to take in performing with other musicians must have overridden any other artistic or financial considerations. Any time Williams spends with the Pops and away from film composing probably represents a financial loss for him' (Pfeifer 1982). Orchestra members and music critics voiced their satisfaction with Williams at the helm of the Pops: 'He has brought in a different, more sophisticated, more upgraded approach both to the repertoire and to the treatment of the music. There is more quality in the Pops today', said concertmaster Emanuel Borok (Dyer 1983: 43). And Richard Dyer reported that 'it's quite an experience to watch him reorchestrate something on the spot, making it at once more effective and tasteful. He is extremely interested in quality of sound, and he continues to reseat the orchestra, seeking to avoid the sheer noise and acoustical slapback of some previous Pops experiments' (Dyer 1983: 43) – see Figure 7.

Yet, some rumours had circulated about Williams being unsatisfied: 'there has been speculation for more than a year that this would be his last season with the Pops. Although his tenure was considered a total success . . . the composer . . . was said to be unhappy. He was apparently discontented with the workload and insufficient rehearsal time to prepare new pieces' (Pfeifer 1982).

Despite these minor rumours, Boston woke up on 13 June 1984 to Williams's abrupt resignation, announced in a brief press statement and motivated by 'artistic and creative differences between myself and the orchestra' (Ford & Impemba 1984). This had the effect of a bombshell, a shock for everyone: for the musicians, taken aback by the firm act of protest; for the BSO management, who suddenly risked the embarrassment of having no leader for the 100th anniversary of the orchestra next year; for Bostonians, who had embraced the new conductor. It was registered as a much serious development:

> The Boston Pops podium is looked upon with a gravity equal to that of its parent Boston Symphony Orchestra – maybe more, because of its wide-ranging concert-hall and recordings audiences. Thus, when Pops conductor John Williams announced last week that he would walk away from his job at the end of the current season, the news was greeted with as much alarm as if BSO's music director Seiji Ozawa were to do the same thing. (Safford 1984)

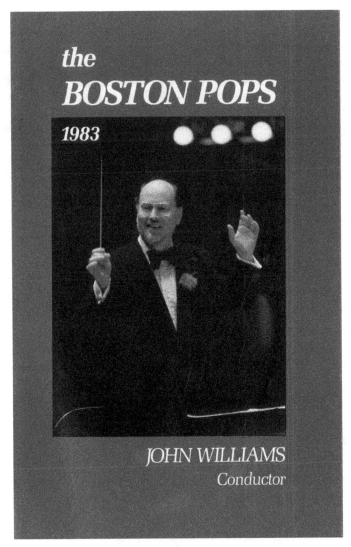

Figure 7 Cover of the programme booklets of the 1983 Pops season, right after Williams's contract renewal (Courtesy BSO Archives, used by permission)

Speculations and leaked information soon ran in local and national newspapers as to what exactly was behind the 'Popsgate'. According to a widely spread rumour, during the rehearsal of 12 June there was some hissing directed at a new Williams piece, *America, the Dream Goes On* (Gorfinkle 1984a). The account of Pops' First Clarinet, Pasquale Cardillo, was the lengthiest:

> Cardillo says it was the first time in Williams' tenure with the orchestra that
> he had conveyed his unhappiness to the orchestra not only with events of that

morning, but with their musicianship in the past. 'He's never gotten angry' says Cardillo, 'He never said a harsh word on the stage to anybody. It was close to intermission. He stopped the orchestra because there was talking going on. There was inattentiveness. People were supposed to be playing. I knew it was noisy. He said two things. We hadn't played "The Raymond Overture" well. He was upset about that. And he was also upset about "Varsity Drag." He went on to discuss his role as a conductor. But the event that was to culminate in Williams's resignation came after the twenty-minute intermission. The orchestra returned and played Williams's own composition "America the Dreams Goes On." When it was concluded there was hissing from some unidentified orchestra members. . ..' Cardillo says that only two or three, 'five at the most', were involved in the hissing. (Stewart 1984)

Other sources said that 'a player hissed', adding mystery to the amount of participation in the incident (Gorfinkle 1984b). Right at the end of the 13 June concert, the entire orchestra convened backstage to offer their apologies to Williams, to no avail (Lumsden 1984). Williams declined to elucidate the reason for his resignation, and more speculations mounted in the newspaper: 'Rumors about Williams' displeasure over player decorum here had surfaced in previous seasons and in July 1981 came the first printed reports that he had serious questions about renewing his contract' (Miller 1984a). The alleged hissing was increasingly revealed as only the tip of a much deeper iceberg, 'the straw that broke the camel's back' (Gorfinkle 1984a).

In the following days, more reports emerged, revealing a history of long-standing demotivated attitude and carelessness on the part of the orchestra members during rehearsals, a pattern of bad behaviour that had been a constant with Fiedler (Miller 1984a). The orchestra was thus exposed to the public opinion as a sort of dysfunctional family, 'always ambivalent about the Pops, the BSO players became increasingly resentful. . ... The audience always had a good time, but there was little joy onstage. The attitude of the musicians bothered Fiedler, and he complained about it constantly, but he soldiered on, even through years of increasingly fragile health' (Dyer 1985: 12). Such was the contempt for the Pops repertoire that a custom had consolidated: 'The player hissing as they began rehearsing new music – novelties and arrangements of show tunes – that Maestro Arthur Fiedler used to commission for the festive final third of a Pops program' (Miller 1984b). The hissing, then, was apologetically attributed by some to this notorious habit, not personally aimed at Williams, in an attempt to minimise the incident. Some in the orchestra tried to defuse the negative publicity, stating that attitude had nothing to do with Williams's resignation – 'John was very well accepted by the orchestra. There seemed to be a good rapport. The discipline with John was 1000-percent better than it was with Fiedler', said Cardillo (Stewart 1984). Others acknowledged that the orchestra's deteriorated behaviour had a role in the crisis: 'Craig Nordstrom, chairman of the Players' Committee, representing all Boston Symphony Orchestra members, said he thinks the musicians "have awakened" to possible discipline problems by Williams' action. . ... Asked if the orchestra is embarrassed, Nordstrom said, "Yes, there is a feeling of embarrassment and we're sorry that it happened"' (Miller 1984a). Others reported that the musicians considered Williams a '"stickler for musical detail" who has a "fine sense of orchestral balance" and is "committed to excellence"' (Ford & Impemba 1984). This sounds like a compliment, prima facie, but it might be also revelatory as to the 'creative differences' that Williams mentioned as the cause of his stepping down, the actual motive besides the 'traditional' hissing. Some musicians in the orchestra might think that the popular repertoire was not worth 'stickling for detail' and did not warrant a commitment to excellence.

The incident disclosed the prejudice that had existed in a more or less veiled fashion from the beginning of Williams's tenure. If members of the orchestra had long had little tolerance and a lack of dedication for popular music, being 'forced' to play popular music – and now increasingly *film* music – under the baton of a Hollywood composer was probably adding insult to injury for some of them. In a recent podcast interview, Leonard Slatkin seemed to confirm this: 'Some of the musicians just didn't respect someone who came from that world. . ... It was all about how the orchestra was treating him. He didn't expect to be treated any differently from any other conductor that stood in front of the Boston Symphony' (Score Masters: Celebrating John Williams and Jerry Goldsmith: 01.26.00). A former orchestra member, remarking how the first chairs of the Boston Symphony were free not to play in the Pops, commented: 'The stars of the BSO, the principals or section leaders, are not part of the Pops but make up the Boston Symphony Chamber Players, who fulfill a musician's fondest dreams of playing chamber music while colleagues are playing "Star Wars"' (Speyer 1984). To some, one of the innovations Williams brought to the repertoire, film music, was no less debasing than Fiedler's 'trashy arrangements'. Part of the press showed a prejudicial stance in their explanations for Williams's departure, laying bare an implicit distrust of the Hollywood composer and rehashing the 'money versus art' argument. For example, 'Cardillo believes that Williams used an incident on Tuesday, June 12 as a lever to do what he long has wanted to do – quit the Pops' (Stewart 1984). And why would Williams quit the Pops? The venal motive is alleged in another article: 'A source close to the orchestra said Williams ... may move to the West Coast to be closer to the lucrative film offers' (Ford & Impemba 1984), because, argued another source, 'he is also a multimillionaire ... and can pick and choose what he wants to do and where he wants to be. He no longer wants to be in Boston and conduct the Pops' (Bass 1984). Commenting on Williams's reaction to the hissing, another music critic wrote: 'This was more than a businessman-artist like Williams could take, obviously. Chin waggers had been talking since his second summer of the conductor's loss of patience. Finally, wealthy and busy enough anyway, he said, "Nuts, I don't need it," or words to that effect, and quit' (Safford 1984). If already this article seems to put the blame on Williams's supposed businessman-like lack of patience, worries that had already been raised at the time of his appointment were recalled: he was not a conductor but a film composer. 'There are significant differences between making music at the Pops and in a Hollywood recording studio. Williams may be used to something the Pops has never been. Recording a film score is the model of efficiency' (Speyer 1984). According to these analyses, the problem was not so much the orchestra as the fact that Williams had never been really suitable to the job: he was a Hollywood composer, a 'businessman-artist', and a 'wealthy' one with no time or patience to lose on music-making less profitable than Hollywood assignments. *Boston Herald*'s Larry Katz pinpointed the issues whose solution the orchestra could not postpone any more:

> Williams resigned because he was in a no-win situation: He couldn't please the fun-loving Pops audience and the musically expert Pops orchestra at the same time. Though the Pops management would like to keep it a secret, the truth is that, by and large, the members of the orchestra don't like playing Pops music. They'd rather be doing something else. But they don't have a choice. ... This has been going on for years, the musicians loathed the Pops when Fiedler was in charge, but Arthur, a former orchestra member himself, was wise to their games and didn't give a hoot about their griping. Fiedler could handle them. But Williams took the hissing personally. ... Now the Pops will look around for a new conductor charming enough to please the masses and thick-skinned enough to ignore the barbs of the orchestra, and maybe the Pops will continue rolling along much as it did before – a money-making but artistically dubious offering to the musically unsophisticated. ... What the Pops really needs is a conductor with enough guts to remake it in a new image. A conductor determined to find a way to please the Pops' audience AND the orchestra, too. A conductor who will give the Pops an artistic as well as a financial and social reason for existing. (Katz 1984)

Unbeknownst to Katz, the conductor he was envisioning for the Pops' future was Williams himself. On 3 August the newspapers announced a surprising twist: Williams had withdrawn his resignation. While rumours and interpretations were circulating in the past month, Williams had kept working unobtrusively in the background:

> Just after he announced his resignation, he asked the players to meet with him. ... The meetings, with all 100 members of the orchestra were unprece-dented. 'Conductors and orchestra members don't as a rule talk openly to one other', said Craig Nordstrom, chairman of the players committee. 'That's

where I learned how important the Pops was to him. Up till then, I thought
conducting the Pops for him was just another feather in the cap of a celebrity',
said bassist Lawrence Wolfe. (Gorfinkle 1984b)

The meetings proved fruitful and Williams 'had come to terms with the
musicians', thus making him reconsider his resignation. In Williams's
words, 'the adversity brought out the best in everybody. For the first time,
all of us – the orchestral players, (Boston Symphony Orchestra music
director) Seiji Ozawa, the management, myself – got together and did a lot
of talking. In the past few weeks, these talks have brought out a lot of gripes
and problems that wouldn't have come out otherwise' (Cariaga 1984). The
principal gripe was the mandatory participation of the BSO musicians (apart
from the first chairs) in the Pops season (Gorfinkle 1984b). The other was the
heavy schedule (twelve weeks of six concerts a week plus album recording
sessions, right after the end of the long BSO symphonic season) and, as
Williams put it, 'the tendency in certain quarters . . . to think of the Pops as
a money-making machine: the resulting schedule means that everyone is
overworked' (Dyer 1984), to which he added, 'we all have to remember,
these are artists. The orchestra is not a music factory' (Cariaga 1984). The
Boston Pops conductor also shed some light on the incident and provided the
reasons for his resignation: 'The events of last spring may have been a little
misunderstood, and that's partly my fault, for my unreadiness to talk about
them. But I feel that these were private things, family things, if you will, not
appropriate to talk about, and really beneath the dignity of a great orchestra'
(Cariaga 1984), and he denied the rumours that had been spread: 'My friends
in California read the papers and kept asking me why I put up with people
flying paper airplanes and throwing spitballs. Well, I wouldn't. And never
did – I simply never experienced that sort of behavior. What was widely
reported as a problem of discipline was really a problem of morale' (Dyer
1984). He would later specify that, 'our differences had to do with attitude'
(Christy 1989). The 'artistic and creative differences' between Williams and
the orchestra were about the different views of popular music: for Williams, 'The
high point of my music year is coming to Boston. . . .. To them, it's playtime, but to
me it's serious. I wanted to express my musical goals pretty high' (Goodman 1986).

Improvements came in the form of a series of changes that Williams
launched in order to address the concerns and complaints raised during the
meetings, all aimed at making orchestra members more gratified when playing
in the Pops. He confessed: 'I hope the situation has been better than it was
during the last years of Arthur Fiedler's tenure, but obviously it isn't good
enough yet. I am not deceiving myself into thinking that everybody is going to

be happy all the time. What is important is that what we do is good, relevant, fun, and always improving' (Dyer 1984). One of such improvements was to make the table service during the concerts less noisy and distracting. Lights were also dimmed so as to promote a more focussed musical experience for the patrons (Dyer 1993: 35). The biggest innovation to increase the musicians' motivation was a new clause that, starting from the new 1987 contract, would allow BSO players to opt not to play in the Pops, thus reshaping the orchestra into a more motivated and cohesive group (Gorfinkle 1984c). Williams also continued and intensified his policy of looking for musically satisfying new commissions and arrangements, so as to keep the musicians interested and challenged, following his belief that all music can be good music, regardless of its genre – 'There is far more difference between playing a Haydn symphony and a Richard Strauss tone poem than between playing a Strauss tone poem and a Duke Ellington arrangement' (Dyer 1984). For Williams, 'playing the Pops is good for the Boston Symphony if it's not a clown thing that degrades the orchestra. Our dignity and musical integrity can be kept' (Katz 1985). He further discussed his view:

> The question has been whether it is appropriate for classical trained musicians to play popular music, and at what point playing Pops becomes damaging for an ensemble whose principal function is to perform the classics. In the past couple of months, the players have demonstrated renewed commitment to the Pops as a part of the BSO's musical mission. I think there is agreement that playing the Pops can be a healthy part of our musical life if we handle it well, if we do it well. As musicians, the real issue always is how well we are doing, whether we can be proud of what we do. The most important thing for all of us is to leave the stage feeling as if we had done our best. (Dyer 1985: 13)

He confessed that,

> the biggest thrill I've gotten out of Boston is when some players have come to me after the season and said, "That was great, we had a real stretch, and the brass players had a wonderful blow, and we got to Tanglewood in better shape than ever before, because of what the Pops repertoire was able to do for us." That is the biggest praise I could get. (Katz 1985)

The advantage of an orchestra that plays both the 'classical' and the popular repertoire is, to Williams, a higher degree of versatility that can be beneficial also when playing art music:

> The Boston Symphony is one of the five or six great orchestras in the country. I've conducted most of the others, and none of them can do what the BSO does because they've been called upon to play many musical styles. Does

playing for Pops help them to play Mozart? My opinion is that stylistic breadth in the repertoire has to have a benefit. (Gorfinkle 1985)

Having taken place right on the threshold of the orchestra's 100th anniversary, 'Williams resignation was a very serious matter' and it had the effect of 'a serious reevaluation of the Pops and of the procedures that support and direct it' (Dyer 1985: 13). In retrospect, it seems it was a move on Williams's part to gain some leverage in order to obtain those changes that the orchestra had been awaiting for long, and to reaffirm his commitment to the popular repertoire – including film music – at the helm of an orchestra that should be as serious and as committed as he was.

After the felicitous solution of the 'Popsgate', Williams led the Pops for another nine seasons, leaving the position at the end of the 1993 season to concentrate more on composition and private life (Dyer 1991a). Williams continued to collaborate and make regular appearances with the orchestra as their 'Laureate Conductor'. If in his first decade at the Pops Williams pioneered the presentation of the film-music repertoire alongside the 'proper' concert-music repertoire, in the final years of his tenure – and in the 'Laureate Conductor' follow-up – Williams specialised in the experimentation of multimedia presentations of film music.

7 The Boston Pops and Multimedia

In the introduction, I have mentioned the topicality of multimedia films or cine-concerts. Williams was a pioneer of such multimedia combinations of projected sound films and live music, and conducted some memorable and adventurous early experiments, which achieved a wide visibility because of the Pops' concerts and television presence.[32] Early signals of this interest can be traced back to his very first press conference as newly appointed conductor of the Boston Pops, in which Williams declared his intention to 'experiment with electronic and mixed-media music' (Swan et al. 1980: 86). In a 1981 interview he expressed his vision of 'music and film combined, a sort of new symphonic device', and he seemed to foresee the diffusion of today's multimedia films: 'I saw the most amazing thing in London. It was Abel Gance's great silent film, *Napoléon*. ... It is playing in London with a soundtrack of classical music, Beethoven, Brahms, ... I know that it is supposed to be unnecessary to combine music with vision, almost tasteless. But this is the way a movie should look and sound!' (Montgomery 1981).

The first attempt to combine music and film clips can be traced back to the inaugural show of the 1983 season of the TV show *Evening at Pops* – titled 'John

---

[32] Williams was preceded in these experiments by Maurice Jarre in the 1992 concert 'David Lean Tribute' at London's Royal Albert Hall (*Maurice Jarre: A Tribute to David Lean*, directed by L.A. Johnson, DVD, Milan Records, 2007, M2-36317) and by John Mauceri conducting a multimedia concert with the National Symphony Orchestra in the same year (Kendall 1992b). Yet, Williams's multimedia presentations were more regular and more influential because of their high visibility.

Williams Special'.[33] Williams and producer William Cosel decided to have some musical pieces coupled with video inserts: 'We want to break with the traditional concert format on TV . . .. Instead of a straight performance show, we decided to experiment with one visual show', explained Cosel (Rothemberg 1983). In the show, Williams's choral piece 'Gloria', from the film *Monsignor* (1982, dir. Frank Perry) was illustrated by bucolic views of the Berkshire hills, and footage from the Norman Rockwell Museum in Stockbridge, MA, was coupled with Chaplin's 'Smile' from *Modern Times*. The original idea was to provide other entries of the programme with video clips too, including the 'Flying Theme' from *E.T. the Extraterrestrial* and Paul Dukas's *L'apprenti sorcier* (*The Sorcerer's Apprentice*) coupled with the famous Walt Disney visualisation from *Fantasia* (1940). The footage of the latter 'was too expensive [to license] and did not synchronize properly with the Pops version', while for the former 'a request [had been put in] to Steven Spielberg for clips from *E.T.* but [we] never heard from him' (Rothemberg 1983). Cosel, though, was resolute that he and Williams 'would still like to occasionally do more interpretative, visual pieces – and do them better' (Rothemberg 1983). In 1990 Spielberg proved more collaborative and even hosted an entire show called 'Spielberg Special', in which music from his films was coupled with visuals.[34] These two *Evening at Pops* episodes were not live multimedia events – there was no projection during the live concert – but only audio-visual coupling made in post-production. Yet, they can be considered the first extensive audiovisual presentations of film music attempted by Williams.

The first truly multimedia live presentation occurred in 1993, during 'A Gala Celebration of John Williams', the opening night of Williams's last season as Pops conductor. In the central part of the concert, the actor Richard Dreyfuss hosted a selection titled 'Composing for Film: A Behind the Scenes Look'. The barrel chase sequence from *Jaws* (1975, dir. Steven Spielberg) was first screened without the music track – with dialogue and sound effects only. Then, the same sequence was rerun with Williams conducting the orchestra live to film. After that, a second multimedia piece was offered: an eight-minute medley combining live music from *Star Wars* ('Main Title'), *Raiders of the Lost Ark* ('Escape from the Temple'), *Jaws* ('Theme'), *Superman: the Movie* ('The Flying Sequence'), *Star Wars* ('The Binary Sunset'), *E.T.* ('Bicycle Chase and Finale'), with the projection of clips from the related films.[35] The two multimedia pieces presented in the 12 May 1993 concert are representative examples of the two multimedia formats which Williams would further develop in the following years, 'multimedia film piece' and 'multimedia concert piece'

[33] WGBH Media Library and Archives: *Evening at Pops* #EAP-19-83.
[34] WGBH Media Library and Archives: *Evening at Pops* #1302.
[35] WGBH Media Library and Archives: *Evening at Pops* #1601 R.

(Audissino 2014a, 2014b), respectively. The 'multimedia concert piece', exemplified by the medley presented in the 12 May 1993 concert, is a concert piece adapted from a film score (in the form of an overture, medley, suite, etc. . . .) accompanied by projected film clips that can be said to illustrate the music. Some examples of multimedia concert pieces presented by Williams over the years are *Selections from Psycho*; *Selections from Lawrence of Arabia*; *Excerpts from Close Encounters of the Third Kind*; *The Busby Berkeley Years* – a medley of Harry Warren's music for Busby Berkeley's films; a medley from *Dr. Zhivago*; the prelude from *North by Northwest*; a medley combing the 'Einleitung' from Richard Strauss's *Also Sprach Zarathustra* with Johann Strauss Jr.'s *An der schönen blauen Donau* accompanied by clips from *2001: a Space Odyssey* (1968, dir. Stanley Kubrick); *Monsters, Beauties and Heroes* – a medley arranged by Williams and featuring music from *King Kong* (1933, dir. Ernest B. Schoedsack and Merian C. Cooper, music by Max Steiner), *Jaws*, *Casablanca*, *An Affair to Remember* (1957, dir. Leo McCarey, music by Hugo Friedhofer), *The Adventures of Robin Hood*, and *Superman: the Movie* (1978, dir. Richard Donner, music by John Williams); *Hooray for Hollywood*, a three and a half minute Williams arrangement of the same-name Richard Whiting song from *Hollywood Hotel* (1937, dir. Busby Berkeley), accompanied by a visual anthology of Hollywood cinema, from *Blood and Sand* (1922, dir. Fred Niblo), to *Some Like It Hot* (1959, dir. Billy Wilder); Max Steiner's *Casablanca* suite, accompanied by a montage featuring the film's most iconic scenes. The 'multimedia film piece' – exemplified by the *Jaws* excerpt presented in the 12 May 1993 concert – is an entire scene or sequence from a given film, comprising of dialogue and sound effects, that is accompanied live with the same music featured in the film. This is the antecedent of today's 'cine-concerts', representing early experiments in the combination of projected video, pre-recorded dialogue, and sound-effects with live music. The level of synchronisation here is higher than in the multimedia concert piece because any slippage that might occur between music and visuals would be more evident in this live reenactment of the film than in the other, illustrative-only format.

The main difficulty for multimedia concerts had been technology, and in the 1990s technical innovations had started making things increasingly easier.[36] On

---

[36] The following are some technical aids used to conduct to film. One system is aural, the click-track, a guiding sound track that keeps an orchestra in synchronisation with a film: the conductor and players wear headphones in which they hear a metronome-like pulse (click, click, click . . .) that, if strictly followed, makes the musical performance adhere to the visual flow. The relentless and rigid pulse has the tendency of straight-jacketing the music into a mechanical performance. The others are visual aids, the streamers and punches, which provide a less constrictive guidance. Punches are holes that used to be made in the film strip at regular intervals, resulting in a series of

the occasion of a *Star Wars* multimedia medley that Williams presented in 1997 for the film's twentieth anniversary, some technicalities were detailed:

> First, the planners had to get permission from Steven Spielberg and George Lucas to 'edit out some of the scenes from their movies that show what music can contribute', Williams explained. Then the composer had to extract the music from those scenes and stitch the excerpts together in a musically and dramatically cohesive way. 'You have to make sure there are no musical bumps', whether harmonic, orchestral or melodic. After doing this 'cut-and-paste' work, Williams and his editors go back over the roughly eight-minute first draft and see how it plays, then rearrange segments if necessary to make everything flow better. Then, there may be more musical editing. Once the draft version is complete, Williams has to extract the individual orchestral parts from the complete score and get them printed. . ... For Williams, there is also a videotaped version of the film excerpts with precisely marked cues projected on a small monitor so he can conduct the music in synchronization with the images. (Pfeifer 1997)

Even with all the supporting synchronisation technology, someone skilled in conducting to film is needed. Such a task requires a significant amount of practice as it is in contrast with the typical training of conductors, not used to sticking to the unyielding pace imposed by the film projection. Williams demonstrated his mastery of live synch-conducting with some multimedia film pieces from Hollywood musicals in which the level of synchronism reached the peak of virtuosity. In a sort of reverse-engineering operation, it is not the dancers to dance to the music but the orchestra to play to the dancers. What makes these dance multimedia film pieces particularly remarkable is precisely the 'high-wire stunt' quality of the virtuoso synch-playing. An instance was presented in a 1996 concert televised in the *Evening at Pops* series, with Stanley Donen as a special guest.[37] Multimedia film pieces included the umbrella dance from *Singin' in the Rain* (1952, dir. Stanley Donen, Gene

---

white flashes that communicated the pulse to follow in order to keep the synchronisation – a visual version of the click-track. Streamers are even less intruding: a diagonal line was traced across the filmstrip leading to the frame with a synch-point to be hit musically – for example, a stab to be mirrored by a blast of the brass. The synch-point frame was punched with a hole. The visual effect for the conductor is a white line that crosses the screen from left to right, usually taking two seconds, at the end of whose journey a white dot flashes. The appearance of the line on the left side alerts the conductor that a synch-point is approaching, which is to be hit exactly when the line touches the right side, on the appearance of the white flash. These visual aids are paired with matching markings on the score: a horizontal line above the measures quantifies the length covered by the streamer's journey, and the line terminates with an X mark, which indicates the synch-point and coincides with the white flash. Nowadays both the streamers and punches are superimposed digitally with time-processor software like The Auricle. In the recording studio these visual aids are visible on the big screen above the orchestra; in concerts they are only displayed on the conductor's LCD monitor.

[37] WGBH Media Library and Archives: *Evening at Pops* #1905.

Kelly, music by Arthur Freed and Nacio Herb Brown); Gene Kelly's roller-skating dance from *It's Always Fair Weather* (1955, dir. Stanley Donen, Gene Kelly, music by André Previn, Betty Comden, Adolph Green); the dance duet between Kelly and Jerry Mouse from *Anchors Aweigh* (1945, dir. George Sidney, music by Sammy Fain and Arthur Freed), Fred Astaire's ceiling dance from *Royal Wedding* (1951, dir. Stanley Donen, music by Burton Lane and Alan Jay Lerner); Cyd Charisse's 'The Desert Song' from *Deep in My Heart* (1954, dir. Stanley Donen); and the barn dance from *Seven Brides for Seven Brothers* (1954, music by Johnny Mercer and Gene de Paul, dir. Stanley Donen) – see Figure 8.

This last piece, the 'Barn Dance', was particularly spectacular and demanding: the tempo is fast, music runs for six and a half minutes without a pause, and there are fifty-nine explicit synch-points to be precisely hit by the orchestra, which also has to maintain the right tempo so that the steps and gyrations of the complex on-screen choreography match the flow of the live music performance. The composer and arranger Angela Morley was amongst the attendees:

> They put them on the screen one after the other and John just chased them with the orchestra and – boy! – it was the most immaculate synch! I don't know how that could be done. Nobody had headphones, ... there was no clicks lying around. All John was doing was looking at streamers and looking at the clock. And, you know, there is some tricky moment. In the dance on the ceiling, Fred Astaire suddenly goes [*she demonstrates by tapping an irregular rhythmic pattern on the chair's armrest*], something like that, and it has to be right on the beat! ... And then there's the roller-skating routine in *It's Always Fair Weather*. There's a place where he slows down and then he speeds up, I mean, there's some little tempo changes, you know, that has to be exactly right. It's beyond me to understand anybody who has that kind of skill.[38]

Other examples of such live-conducting dexterity were televised in a 2001 *Evening at Pops* episode, where Williams conducted a medley of the Nicholas Brothers' tap-dance numbers,[39] and in a 2003 *Evening at Pops* episode, which featured the opening 'Train Chase Sequence' from *Indiana Jones and the Last Crusade* (dir. Steven Spielberg, 1989).[40] This is a complex sequence running five minutes and fifteen seconds, 'almost like a circus ballet piece. ... There are about 50 or more musical sync points. ... It's very compressed, very tight and very quick', Williams commented (Anon. 2006: 98).

---

[38] Angela Morley, 'Angela Morley in Private Interview, 1999', video, YouTube, https://youtu.be/A3Xb9XDDeAo, 00.36.00–00.38.00, accessed 5 October 2021.

[39] WGBH Media Library and Archives: *Evening at Pops* #2501.

[40] WGBH Media Library and Archives: *Evening at Pops* #2705.

Figure 8 John Williams conducting the Stanley Donen multimedia film pieces
(note the monitor feeding the visual synch-marks next to the podium).
Screengrabs from *Evening at Pops*, #1905, 18 May 1996

These various multimedia experiments presented in concert were the technical trial field for the live accompaniment of entire film, those 'cine-concerts'
that are now featured worldwide. If the first examples of such multimedia films
were silent-cinema revivals – Abel Gance's *Napoléon* (1927) in the 1980s
(Brownlow 1983: 237–40) – an influential benchmark demonstration for
sound films was again presided over by Williams. On 16 March 2002, upon

the twentieth anniversary of *E.T. The Extraterrestrial*, Williams conducted the Recording Arts Orchestra of Los Angeles live to the film, in what Universal Pictures' press statement called 'the first time in history a non-silent film has been presented in its entirety with live full orchestral accompaniment'.[41] If not an absolute 'first', the primacy of the *E.T.* event cannot be understated. Live accompaniment of sound films had been attempted and presented before: André Previn had conducted Prokofiev's score for *Alexander Nevsky* (1935, dir. Sergei Eisenstein) live to picture in 1987 (McCorkle Okazaki 2020: 7–8), and closer to 2002, on 24 and 26 May 2001, Howard Shore conducted his own scores with the London Philharmonic in a live accompaniment to *Dead Ringers* (1988, dir. David Cronenberg) and *Naked Lunch* (1991, dir. David Cronenberg) (Anon. 2001). The influential importance of the *E.T.* multimedia event lies not in its being *the* first, but in its being the first to succeed in such a complex audiovisual live combination. Compared to the two Cronenberg films and to *Alexander Nevsky*, *E.T.* was a substantially bigger challenge. Firstly, its score is much more pervasive: the music practically covers the entire film. Secondly, the *E.T.* score calls for a considerably higher degree of minute synchronism between music and visuals – despite Eisenstein's much touted *Nevsky* audiovisual diagrams – and the musical performance is required to be much more precise in tempi, much more tight in adherence to visuals, and much more accurate in its interaction with the pre-recorded dialogue and sound effects than in the Prokofiev and Shore examples. *E.T.* demanded the virtuoso synch-playing that Williams had long trained for with such multimedia pieces as the 'Barn Dance', now extended to the entire duration of a musically rich film. Williams explained that it was:

> like doing a two-hour opera without an intermission and without a chance to adjust anything. The film is exactly, metrically, unyieldingly what it is. So the timing must be either completely right or it's totally wrong. . .. We have to go through the whole two hours mathematically, trying to make the orchestra exactly in synch with the action and the dialogue as it is supposed to be.[42]

Moreover, the *E.T.* event had larger visibility in the press and it was video-taped and later included in the DVD release of the twentieth-anniversary edition, which gave the event a primacy in terms of diffusion, making an exemplary case of it. It was the culmination of all the experiments in live-accompaniment that Williams had performed with the Boston Pops.

---

[41] Terry Curtin, press statement, Universal Pictures, 31 January 2002.

[42] John Williams in the documentary *Live at the Shrine! John Williams and the World Premiere of E.T.* (2002, dir. Laurent Bouzereau).

8 Film Music after Williams's Tenure

At the end of Williams's tenure in 1994, the initial goal of bringing film music to
the limelight had been achieved on multiple fronts: film-music albums; recon-
structions of the original orchestrations of some of the Hollywood classics; the
now-regular presence of the film-music repertoire in the concert programmes;
film music showcased in three US national tours and three oversea tours to Japan,
as well as on nationwide television shows that reached an audience of four million
viewers (Paiste 1993).[43] Richard Dyer commented that Williams, 'brought his
own missionary zeal to the cause of film music, and not just his own. Some people
complained that he played too much of his own music; but when he didn't put
some of his own music on a program, more people complained that he hadn't'
(Dyer 1993: 34), and he maintained that, 'Williams' importance is that he has
constantly reminded us that lasting popular success is not incompatible with high
artistic standards' (Dyer 1991b). Williams led the orchestra in the 1994 transition
season and participated in the search for a successor (Dyer 1994), appointed in
1995: Keith Lockhart. In a paper delivered at the 1996 Pops symposium of the
National Conference of American Symphony Orchestra League, Lockhart demonstrated to share Williams's philosophy:

> What we have to do is dedicate ourselves to doing work on pops concert that we
> can all be proud of as artists and as people who believe passionately in the
> arts. . . . There are qualitative benchmarks and parameters we should use when
> deciding what we should present as being the best work of our orchestra. . . .
> People want to hear good music. They want to hear intellectually and emotion-
> ally challenging music. When they go to the Pops, though, perhaps it's because
> they want to hear it in a slightly different venue, with a slightly different
> feeling – the feeling that they are released to enjoy it, not the feeling that
> they are being exposed to it in a reverential sort of way. It's important, of
> course, to mix and match very carefully. But the great thing about pops concerts
> is that they don't have those inherent boundaries stuck between them, those
> ways of defining what a concert should be. (Lockhart 1996: 30, 61)

Some wording is quite significant in Lockhart's address: the overturn of the
'reverential' attitude that Romantic aesthetics had injected in the concert-going
practice; being 'proud' about quality; the role of pops concerts in the disintegration of 'boundaries' between one musical genre and the other, including that
between film music and concert music. Under Lockhart's tenure, film music has
remained a fixture of the Pops programmes, despite a slight tendency to return to
the third part – see Figure 9.

---

[43] Statistics of the Williams tenure are provided in the concert booklet of 'Opening Night at Pops.
A Gala Celebration for John Williams', 12 May 1993 (Boston Symphony Archives), 55–63.

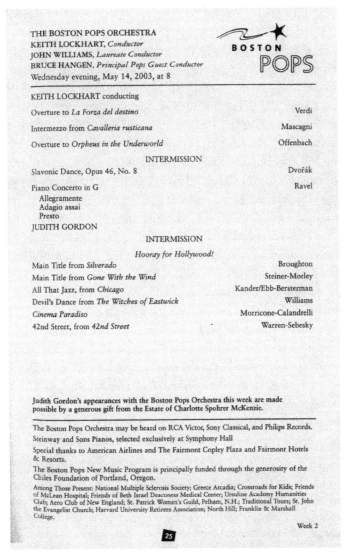

Figure 9 Film music in Keith Lockhart's programmes, 14 May 2003
(Courtesy BSO Archives, used by permission)

After Williams, multimedia presentations too have become a staple of
Boston Pops concerts. On 25 May 2005 Bruce Hangen presented Darius
Milhaud's *Le Boeuf sur le toit*, op. 58 in synchronisation with the short film
Caught in a Cabaret (1914, dir. Charles Chaplin and Mabel Normand).[44] In

---

[44] *Le Boeuf sur le toit* is also titled 'Cinematographic Symphony on South American Tunes'
because it was originally conceived as an accompaniment for a Charlie Chaplin short film,
though it is not clear which specific Chaplin film it was written for: see Calabretto 2010: 261.

2006 a fixed panoramic screen, covering the entire width of the stage, and a projection system were installed in Symphony Hall, allowing multimedia pieces to be featured regularly in the programmes. Keith Lockhart programmed multimedia presentations of the concert repertoire too, for example, Aaron Copland's *Lincoln Portrait* (6 May 2009), or Gustav Holst's *The Planets* (11 June 2009). For the 2010 season, the orchestra's 125th anniversary, Lockhart commissioned *The Dream Lives On: A Portrait of the Kennedy Brothers* (music by Peter Boyer, texts by Lynn Ahrens) for narrator, chorus, orchestra, and a montage of photographs and archive footage of the Kennedys projected on the screen (18 May 2010). In the 2010s, the Boston Pops seasons have regularly featured entire multimedia films, including world premieres like *Jaws* (25 May 2017) and musicals like *Singin' in the Rain* ('A Symphonic Night at the Movie', 8 May 2015), and Lockhart has established himself as one of the most accomplished conductors for multimedia films (see Audissino & Lehman 2018).

As the orchestra's 'Laureate Conductor', Williams has since made regular appearances each year. In the late 1990s, he increasingly focussed his concerts on the film-music repertoire, and since the year 2000 he almost exclusively specialised in film-music programmes. This coincided with the launch of the 'Film Night at Tanglewood', an annual event conducted by Williams at the Tanglewood Festival in the Berkshires, Massachusetts, the summer home of the Boston Symphony and the Pops – see Figure 10.

Williams's work with the Pops had a ripple effect that engendered changes all over the orchestral world, internationally, as confirmed by Lockhart:

> One of the first things that changed the viewpoint of the way film music was perceived in the broader world of orchestral music was John's appointment here in Boston. That's not his music specifically; it's taking a Hollywood composer seriously enough to give him a position in the world of orchestral music, which is the starchiest and most rigid of all performing arts. I wasn't around here in 1980 but I'm sure that there were people going, 'Well, I wonder what he is just playing . . . Just *that* stuff?'. And without question the answer was to some extent 'not just that stuff', but that's the stuff John knows, not just his own music but Korngold, Waxman, Rózsa . . . All that stuff entered the repertoire, stuff that Fiedler had probably never touched. (Audissino & Lehman 2018: 407)

At least a few instances of such impact should be given. One is America's second Pops orchestra, the Cincinnati Pops, founded in 1977 by Erich Kunzel. Kunzel guest-conducted the Boston Pops thirty-seven times between 1977 and 2009 and was also a short-listed candidate to take up Fiedler's baton in 1979. Following the Williams model, Kunzel intensified the

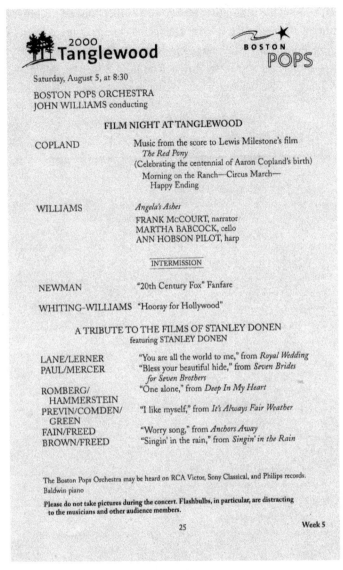

Figure 10 The first 'Film Night' concert at Tanglewood, 5 August 2000
(Courtesy BSO Archives, used by permission)

film-music presentations with the Cincinnati Pops, starting in 1984 with the orchestra's first all-film-music album *Star Tracks* (Telarc – CD-80094). Another cross-over or middlebrow ensemble that was a direct consequence of the Williams/Pops approach was the Hollywood Bowl Orchestra, founded on 17 October 1990 and led by John Mauceri. A Leonard Bernstein pupil, Mauceri had guest-conducted the Boston Pops twenty-six times between 1979

and 1994, making the film-music repertoire a cornerstone of his programmes –
see Figure 11. Mauceri, like Williams, rejected canonical prejudices: 'We can't
go through our lives conducting only the nine symphonies of Beethoven.
There's lots of great music by Erich Korngold and Max Steiner' (Stearns
1991). Mauceri also shared with Williams the same attention to detail:

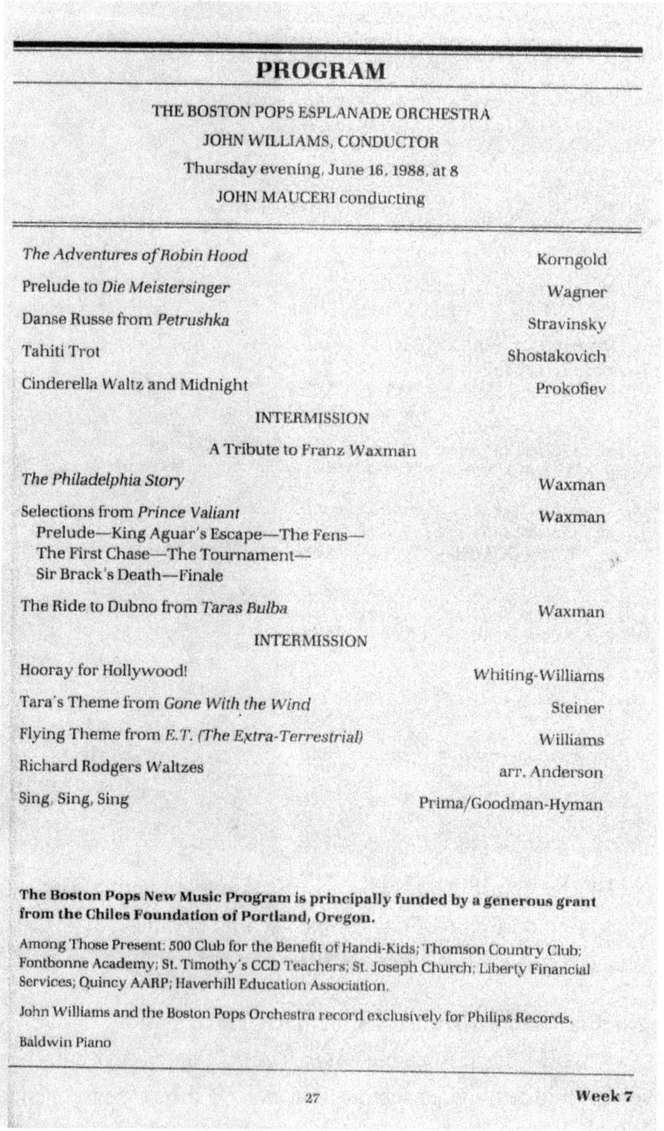

PROGRAM

THE BOSTON POPS ESPLANADE ORCHESTRA
JOHN WILLIAMS, CONDUCTOR
Thursday evening, June 16, 1988, at 8
JOHN MAUCERI conducting

The Adventures of Robin Hood	Korngold
Prelude to Die Meistersinger	Wagner
Danse Russe from Petrushka	Stravinsky
Tahiti Trot	Shostakovich
Cinderella Waltz and Midnight	Prokofiev

INTERMISSION

A Tribute to Franz Waxman

The Philadelphia Story	Waxman
Selections from Prince Valiant Prelude—King Aguar's Escape—The Fens— The First Chase—The Tournament— Sir Brack's Death—Finale	Waxman
The Ride to Dubno from Taras Bulba	Waxman

INTERMISSION

Hooray for Hollywood!	Whiting-Williams
Tara's Theme from Gone With the Wind	Steiner
Flying Theme from E.T. (The Extra-Terrestrial)	Williams
Richard Rodgers Waltzes	arr. Anderson
Sing, Sing, Sing	Prima/Goodman-Hyman

The Boston Pops New Music Program is principally funded by a generous grant from the Chiles Foundation of Portland, Oregon.

Among Those Present: 500 Club for the Benefit of Handi-Kids; Thomson Country Club; Fontbonne Academy; St. Timothy's CCD Teachers; St. Joseph Church; Liberty Financial Services; Quincy AARP; Haverhill Education Association.

John Williams and the Boston Pops Orchestra record exclusively for Philips Records.

Baldwin Piano

27   **Week 7**

Figure 11 Film music in John Mauceri's programmes, 16 June 1988
(Courtesy BSO Archives, used by permission)

'[Mauceri] hunted down the original orchestrations for the film music and recorded it on an MGM soundstage, . . . "And when we're playing the simplest music, we give it as much seriousness of musical intent as any piece of music"' (Stearns 1991).

Esa-Pekka Salonen's conductorship of the Los Angeles Philharmonic (1992–2009) constituted a further contribution to the integration of film music into concert programmes – for example, Salonen's programming and recording of Herrmann's film works. Leonard Slatkin, conductor of Washington's National Symphony Orchestra, teamed up with Williams in 2003 for a film-music festival called 'Soundtrack: Music and Film'. Slatkin explained the scope: 'I want to put film music in a different light, away from the pops programs where it usually gets placed . . . and treat it much the same way as we do excerpts from ballet or opera' (Smith 2003). From 21 January to 1 February, six film-music concerts were offered in in the US capital, as well as conferences and panel discussions. One concert was 'Music and Film: Made in Hollywood, USA' and featured Hollywood's Golden Age composers, while another, 'Music and Film: the European Aesthetic', was devoted to the film works of European composers like Shostakovich, Walton, Prokofiev and Saint-Saëns. One was a multimedia concert, titled 'In Synch: How Do They Do It?', a sort of concert/conference on the specificities of composing for films and on the technicalities of the music/ images synchronisation, with Williams and Slatkin giving practical demonstrations (Lehman 2003). Another act of disintegration of the borders between different categories of music was Andris Nelsons sharing the podium with Williams during the Tanglewood 'Film Night' concerts (19 August 2017 and 11 August 2018), marking the first time that the director of the Boston Symphony crossed over to conduct the Boston Pops in an all-film-music programme.

A few international instances of the breach in the 'iron curtain' that used to separate film music from the 'legitimate' concert repertoire are Zubin Mehta and the Israel Philharmonic recording in 1992 Franz Waxman's *Carmen Fantasy* from his film score for *Humoresque* (1946, dir. Jean Negulesco) alongside music by Paganini and Saint-Saëns; the London the Royal Academy of Music dedicating in 1996 the eleventh edition of the 'International Composers Festival' to film music (16–22 June); Michael Tilson Thomas opening the symphonic season with the San Francisco Symphony Orchestra on 11 September 2004 with a programme featuring Bernard Herrmann's suite from the film *Vertigo* (1958, dir. Alfred Hitchcock) along with Debussy's *La Mer*, Copland's *Danzòn Cubano* and Gershwin's *An American in Paris*; the Gewandhausorchester in Leipzig, Germany, playing film works by Herrmann on 23 January 1998; the Chicago Symphony launching its own series of film-music concerts, 'Friday Night at the Movies', in 2004. In more recent years, Gustavo Dudamel and Stéfane Denève have consistently included film-music entries in their symphonic concerts; the Wiener Philharmoniker programmed a suite from *Star Wars* along with music by Josef Strauss, Liszt and Holst during their annual *Sommernachtskonzert* outdoor concert in the park of the Schönbrunn castle (8 June 2010); Simon Rattle led the Berliner Philharmoniker in a Sommernachtskonzert at the Waldbühne entirely devoted to a programme of Hollywood classics (Bronislau Kaper, Miklós Rózsa, Scott Bradley, Erich Wolfgang Korngold, Jerome Moross, David Raksin, Alfred Newmann, and John Williams), marking the first time that the highly-regarded German orchestra tackled the film-music repertoire this extensively. If one reads through the archives of London's BBC Proms, an increasing presence of film music alongside concert pieces from the canonical repertoire can be noticed, to the point that film music has now become a regular ingredient. For example, in the concert of 10 September 2005 the suite from Korngold's *The Sea Hawk* was presented alongside pieces by Purcell, Handel, and Elgar; in the concert of 24 July 1999 Williams's 'Main Title' from *Star Wars* shared the stage with Haydn, Stravinsky, Prokofiev, Saint-Saëns. A number of special concerts dedicated to the film-music repertoire have also been featured, like 'Hollywood' conducted by Carl Davis on 31 July 1999; the Elmer Bernstein concert on 14 August 2001; the English film-music-themed concert on 14 July 2007; or the numerous appearances of the John Wilson Orchestra.

Audiovisual experiments in concert halls have also seen an increase in number following Williams's examples. In 2002 George Fenton conducted in London his score for the BBC natural history documentary *The Blue Planet* (2001, dir. Alastair Fothergill) in a multimedia live presentation (Cooke 2008: 41). The 1997 celebration concert *The Big Pictures: A Musical Salute to 20th Century Fox* conducted by John Mauceri at the Hollywood Bowl featured both multimedia concert pieces and multimedia film pieces (Bond 1997). Multimedia pieces are now a regular presence at the Hollywood Bowl concerts: for example, in 2001 Mauceri conducted a sci-fi themed concert with both multimedia concert pieces and multimedia film pieces from *Planet of the Apes* (1968, dir. Franklin J. Schaffner, music by Jerry Goldsmith), *Alien*, and *Close Encounters of the Third Kind* (Reid 2001). On 25 May 2004, at the Carnegie Hall, John Barry's score for *The Lion in Winter* (1968, dir. Anthony Harvey) was played accompanied by a projection of clips from the film (Anon. 2004).

Back in 1980, at the time of Williams's appointment, the music critic of the *Cincinnati Enquiry* had written that 'the style and leadership of Fiedler had a great effect on the entire pops field, and Williams will certainly exercise his own influence in the coming years' (Owades 1980). His proved to have been a truthful prevision.

9 Closing Remarks

In the years following Williams's arrival at the Pops, and the consequent wider exposure of the film-music repertoire on the Pops' albums, radio broadcasts, and TV shows, orchestras started to programme it more and more. Film music seems to be now widely accepted as legitimate concert material. Two recent events can be seen as the stamp of approval from the world of 'classical music' of the accomplishments of John Williams, 'the much-maligned composer-conductor' as one reviewer in the 1980s had called him (Moss 1984). Williams was invited on 18 and 19 January 2020 by the Wiener Philharmoniker to conduct two film-music concerts in the Goldener Saal of the Musikverein in Vienna, a veritable 'temple' of 'classical' music, if one had to name one. This was the first time that the prestigious and traditionalist orchestra was conducted by a 'movie composer' in an entire programme of film music. The concert received favourable reviews even from the *Wiener Zeitung* (Irrgeher 2020), what used to be the pulpit of the nineteenth-century musicologist Eduard Hanslick, the strict advocate of Absolute Musik. Williams said that the concert:

> is such a deviation from what they usually do; but they were enormously friendly and warm, and clearly brilliant in their playing. . . . At the intermission of one of the rehearsals, the players came and said to me, 'Maestro, can we play *The Imperial March* (from *Star Wars*)?' . . . I told them I thought I'd already given them too much work for a two-hour concert, and they said, 'well you have, but we want to play *The Imperial March* for you; it's the new *Radetzky*!'. (Beek 2020: 28)

Film music is 'the new *Radetzky*', its consolidated position in the light symphonic repertoire now sanctioned by the Wiener Philharmoniker too.[45] In the same year 2020, on 18 November, Williams was awarded the Gold Medal of London's Royal Philharmonic Society, 'one of the most privileged honours in the world of music'.[46] Launched in 1870, it is 'awarded internationally for the most outstanding musicianship', and its roster of composers, instrumentalists, and conductors includes Johannes Brahms, Sergei Rachmaninov, Richard Strauss, Arturo Toscanini, Serge Prokofiev, William Walton, Igor Stravinsky, Herbert von Karajan, Leonard Bernstein,

---

[45] The 2020 Covid-19 pandemic delayed Williams's debut with the Berliner Philharmoniker to October 2021, with the eighty-nine-year-old composer invited to conduct three all-Williams concerts. In June 2022, Williams is slated to debut at La Scala theatre in Milan, Italy, marking another historic 'first'.

[46] https://royalphilharmonicsociety.org.uk/awards/gold-medal, accessed 19 November 2020.

Pierre Boulez, to name just a few.[47] The motivation for Williams's acceptance into the elite club of the Gold Medalists was him having 'dedicated
his life to ensuring orchestral music continues to speak and captivate
people worldwide' and 'for his shining achievements introducing millions
to orchestral music who may otherwise never have encountered it'.[48] This
medal can be said to be not only in recognition of John Williams the
composer but also of John Williams the conductor and the influential
bridging action of his Boston Pops tenure.

Film music has also been reassessed by music critics. For example,
New Yorker's music critic Alex Ross has recently devoted much space and
attention to Williams (Ross 2018, 2020), and an exemplary testimony of the
change of tide is from *Washington Post*'s Anne Midgette:

> As a classical music critic, I was clueless.... While I liked John Williams's
> music just fine when I first saw the film at age 12, by the time I had attained
> legal adulthood, laden with a cargo of acquired snobbery ..., I had learned,
> and bravely parroted, that 'film music' was somehow beneath me....
> I continued to use 'film music' as a pejorative term that ... probably meant
> to me something akin to 'something which one enjoys, but shouldn't'. This
> isn't a reflection on Williams .... It's a reflection on me, and a reflection on
> the notion of the canon that so many classical music lovers unquestioningly
> embrace. Buying into this hierarchy seemed for years to be an entry-level
> requirement for the kind of life in the arts I hoped to live: initially as a Serious
> Writer With Intellectual Pretensions; later as a classical music critic. Film
> music, and populism, were easy targets. It has taken me half a lifetime to fully
> realize what most people knew at the first hearing: Good means good,
> effective means effective.... My real lesson in learning to admire John
> Williams lay in recognizing yet again the degree to which many of us who
> love the arts, both popular and 'fine', live in silos of our own making, affixing
> labels that have nothing to do with the music and impede our enjoyment of it.
> This is as true for classical fans, looking down their nose in horror at so-called
> pop, as it is for fans of indie-rock who are put off by the supposed elitism of
> the concert hall. (Midgette 2019)

Finally, academia too has been devoting more attention to film music as
music. As I have previously discussed, the most recent theorisation of film
music separated from the film proposes a new modality of fruition called
'cinematic listening' (Long 2008: 7–8), and Frank Lehman has provided
a study of 'film music as concert music' not only as to such reception
modality but also as to how film music is adapted for concert performance.

---

[47] https://royalphilharmonicsociety.org.uk/awards/gold-medal/gold-medal-recipients-since-1870,
accessed 19 November 2020.

[48] https://royalphilharmonicsociety.org.uk/awards/gold-medal/john-williams, accessed 19
November 2020.

Unlike structural listening which, in Lehman's words, 'impels us to seek out coherence at all costs', approaching film music through cinematic listening 'can teach us to stop worrying and celebrate the musically "incoherent" – or better, perhaps, to discover new and more inclusive forms of coherence.... Film-as-concert music ... invites us not to fret over whether music behaves as we expect according to "absolute" expectations; instead, we may take it on its own gloriously contingent terms' (Lehman 2018: 12).

When formulating a framework for the appreciation of film music separated from the film and played in concert, I have found Leonard Meyer's considerations on programme music useful. As with programme music – a symphonic poem like Paul Dukas's *L'apprenti sorcier*, for example, – the listener of film music in concert should embrace what Meyer calls a 'referentialist/expressionist' aesthetic attitude instead of an 'absolutist/formalist' one (Meyer 1956: 1–3).[49] While in the latter Romanticism-influenced mindset the musical value and meaning lie in the music's free form and in its organic self-development, in the former the value of music is also and mainly assessed as to its ability to aptly depict an external reference and transcoding extramusical moods and affective qualities. In Meyer's view:

> a title or program that denotes a particular phenomenon is, in my view, just as much an attribute of a composition as are pitches, durations, and other relationships notated in the score..... It is not merely the purely musical relationships devised by a composer that are innovative, but the relation of these to whatever is considered to be represented by them. (Meyer 1996: 130–1)

Film music is a type of programme music that possesses a particularly intense illustrative and connotative richness, it is 'referential' and 'expressionist' to the maximum. Instead of drawbacks – as seen from an absolutist/formalist viewpoint – these can be embraced as distinguishing and productive traits. In James Wierzbicki's words:

> Whereas the strict modernist/formalist point of view prefers that music's meaning be fully contained within the music itself, the more open aesthetics of film music allows for self-contained expressive devices to co-exist comfortably with material whose meaning derives from associations quite independent of the music itself. Like the formalist composer, the film composer can easily make a 'statement' whose emotive essence involves nothing more than the interplay of consonance and dissonance . . ... Unlike the formalist composer, however, the film composer has always been free to mix purely

---

[49] What Meyer called 'absolutist/formalist' attitude is similar to Lehman's 'structural listening', while 'cinematic listening' is to the 'referentialist/expressionist' attitude.

musical niceties with whatever else might serve a film's dramatic needs. Limited to 'pure' music, the formalist composer perforce deals with matters of tension and release only in an abstract way. Not so restricted, the film composer has license to apply comparable psycho-musical dynamics to material that vis-à-vis a filmic narrative seems somehow concrete. (Wierzbicki 2009: 2–3)

A two-tier criterion to assess the stand-alone quality of film music was offered by Sergio Miceli:

One: the score must have a particularly intense relationship with the visuals. I usually speak of film/music dramaturgy, in the sense that there are typical, specific mechanisms of the film language that do not exist in other languages and music should interpret them through its own language. And here is the other point: this language, beyond the functionality that is often required ... must also give the composer the opportunity to create a structure that has its own musical dignity.. .. And if it has this dignity, a structural idea that governs the composition, then this can be perceived also in relation to the functionality with the images. (Miceli 1999)[50]

To be a good candidate for the concert stage, arguably, film music should fulfil both conditions. Film music in concerts should showcase both those intrinsic musical qualities that we might not have had the chance to appreciate in the competitive sound mix in the film (the composer's musical skills), while at the same time bearing the traces of its functionality by evoking the story, the atmospheres, and the characters from the films (the composer's dramaturgical skills). To evoke a film is not merely a matter of mnemonic associations with some accompanying image – one hears *Yakety Sax* and Benny Hill is instantly visualised while being comically chased in fast-motion by an infuriated mob. Possibly, concert pieces of film music should show that their musical features (Miceli's condition number two) are a direct result of their functionality (Miceli's condition number one). It is a matter of transforming into musical structures and moods the structures and moods of the film. To characterise the aesthetic principle of film music in concert, I find it useful to borrow a concept from film-music scholarship and apply it to film music's concert presentations: 'ancrage' [anchorage]. The term was used by Claudia Gorbman to account for

---

[50] Rai Radio 3 interview of Sergio Miceli, 15 August 1999 (my translation). These Miceli criteria still show some formalistic/idealistic influence: 'musical dignity' and 'structural idea' somewhat remind of the concepts of *Absolute Musik* and Organicism. The important point is not so much the superseding of the formalistic/idealistic categories that characterised the Romantic aesthetics: to some extent, they still survive, even in Williams's own admiration for the Haydn–Mozart–Beethoven–Brahms Canon (Pearson 2012) and in his legitimisation of film music through a heightened attention to its symphonic and formal quasi-*Absolute Musik* qualities. The important point is the discontinuation of the categorical prejudice, the a priori labelling and judging of a category of music before even listening to it.

the signifying power of music in films: 'The musical score's rhythmic, textural, and harmonic qualities, expressive via cultural musical codes, emphasize latent or manifest narrative content through a synergetic relationship with the other channels of filmic discourse. ... Borrowing slightly out of context from Roland Barthes, let us say that music behaves as "ancrage," anchoring the image more firmly in meaning' (Gorbman 1987: 32). Similarly but reversely, the images and moods from the film serve during the concert performance as an ancrage for the formal structures of the musical piece that may otherwise sound arbitrary or musically incongruous, from an absolutist/formalist viewpoint. Consider Ennio Morricone's 'On Earth as It Is in Heaven' from *The Mission* (1986, dir. Roland Joffé). The piece itself can be seen as formally/structurally odd: a Palestrina-like polyphonic motet in Latin, 'Conspectus Tuus', accompanied by harpsichord *obbligato* and pipe organ, is intertwined with a second choir singing the stylistically divergent tune 'Vita Nostra' accompanied by bongos and congas, and in-between a lyrical theme for oboe and strings is inserted, by way of a complex contrapuntal writing – or better, 'modular' writing (Miceli 2009: 625). If the choice may seem inexplicable to the absolutist/formalist who is unaware of the film, to the referentialist/expressionist who is familiar with the film the piece will appear as a masterful musical rendition of the film's theme and plot. The three modules – the Latin motet, the ethnic choir, and the oboe melody – represent the three groups involved in the narrative: the official and Machiavellian Roman Catholic Church; the innocent Guarani indigenous tribe; the compassionate church of father Gabriel, respectively. Another example is Williams's *The Imperial March*, the concert version of 'Darth Vader's Theme' from *The Empire Strikes Back*. From an absolutist/formalist perspective, its structure presents odd and even jolty musical turns. James Buhler has suggested that the peculiar compositional choices – for example, the notable and even forcible avoidance of the dominant-to-tonic movement – reflect the unnatural, artificial technology-led world of the evil Empire depicted in the film, and in particular the theme is a translation in music of the Darth Vader character: formerly a human being, now a inhumane machine (Buhler 2000: 45–8). In a concert, the weird conduct of *The Imperial March* finds a proper explanation if we consider the character/music association. In both the two cases above, the films serve as an ancrage for the musical meaning. We reach a full appreciation of these two pieces if we consider the film/music rapport: the intrinsic 'musical relationships' should be evaluated vis a vis the 'relation of these to whatever is considered to be represented by them', as – and even more than – in programme music.

'Ultimately, the music director of the Boston Pops has a lot to do with the formation of musical taste in America', wrote Richard Dyer about the visibility and influence of that orchestra's podium (Dyer 1980a). The notable increment of presence of film music in concert programmes, the acceptance of its legitimacy by the music-criticism circles, and the increasing academic consideration of the repertoire have all had a significant boost from John Williams's conductorship of the Boston Pops Orchestra. The felicitous union of America's most famous film composer and America's most famous orchestra, both committed to bringing the symphonic sound to the masses, created the ideal condition for film music's legitimization.

Figure 12 John Williams and the Boston Pops Orchestra, 1982 (Photographer unknown. Courtesy BSO Archives, used by permission)

References

Adler, A. W. (2007). 'Classical Music for People Who Hate Classical Music': Arthur Fiedler and the Boston Pops, 1930–1950, Ph.D. Diss, University of Rochester.

Adorno, T. W. & Eisler, H. (2007). *Composing for The Films*, 1947, trans. Graham McCann. London/New York: Continuum.

Altman, R. (2004). *Silent Film Sound*. New York: Columbia University Press.

Anon. (1954). Best-Selling Popular Albums. *Billboard*, 2 October, p. 26.

Anon. (2001). Film Music Concerts. *Film Score Monthly*, January, p. 9.

Anon. (2004). Film Music Concerts. *Film Score Monthly*, March, p. 8.

Anon. (2006). Indiana Jones and the Ultimate Tribute. *Empire*, October, pp. 69–101.

Audissino, E. (2012). John Williams, The Boston Pops Orchestra and Film Music in Concert. In C. D'Alonzo, K. Slock, & P. Dubois, eds., *Cinema, critique des images*. Udine: Campanotto, pp. 230–5.

Audissino, E. (2014a). Overruling a Romantic Prejudice: Forms and Formats of Film Music in Concert Programs. In S. Stoppe, ed., *Film in Concert, Film Scores and their Relation to Classical Concert Music*. Glücksstadt: VWH Verlag, pp. 25–43.

Audissino, E. (2014b). Film Music and Multimedia: An Immersive Experience and a Throwback to the Past. In P. Rupert-Kruse, ed., *Jahrbuch Immersiver Medien 2014: Sounds, Music & Soundscapes*. Marburg: Schüren Verlag, pp. 46–56.

Audissino, E. (2016). Archival Research and the Study of the Concert Presentations of Film Music. The Case of John Williams and the Boston Pops Orchestra. *The Journal of Film Music* 6(2), 147–73.

Audissino, E. (2021). *The Film Music of John Williams. Reviving Hollywood's Classical Style*, 2nd ed. Madison, WI: University of Wisconsin Press.

Audissino, E. & Lehman, F. (2018). John Williams Seen from the Podium. An Interview with Maestro Keith Lockhart. In E. Audissino, ed., *John Williams. Music for Films, Television, and the Concert Stage*. Turnhout: Brepols, pp. 397–408.

Bachman, R. (1989). Behind the Scenes at Evening at Pops. *Nine*, June, pp. 34, 46.

Barnett, K. S. (2010). The Selznick Studio, 'Spellbound', and the Marketing of Film Music. *Music, Sound, and the Moving Image* 4(1), 77–98.

Bass, M. R. (1984). Pops Members Fooling around Said to Blow John Williams's Top. *Berkshire Eagle*, 16 July.

Beek, M. (2020). Maestro of the Movies. *BBC Music Magazine*, December, pp. 26–9.

Benson, R. E. (1999). Charles Gerhardt, 1927–1999. *Film Score Monthly*, April/May, p. 48.

Bernheimer, M. (1983). Pop! John Williams on Philharmonic Podium. *Los Angeles Times*, 12 November.

Bond, J. (1997). Fox Night at the Bowl. *Film Score Monthly*, October, p. 6.

Boston Symphony Orchestra (BSO) (2000). *Boston Pops. The Story of America's Orchestra*. Boston, MA: BSO.

Brownlow, K. (1983). *Napoleon, Abel Gance's Classic Film*. London: Cape.

Buell, R. (1984). At the Pops: Williams' Farewell. *Boston Globe*, 9 July.

Buhler, J. (2000). Star Wars, Music, and Myth. In J. Buhler, C. Flinn, & D. Neumeyer, eds., *Music and Cinema*. Hanover, NH: Wesleyan University Press, pp. 33–57.

Burlingame, J. (2000). From Hollywood to Boston. An Interview with John Williams. In *Boston Pops. The Story of America's Orchestra*, Boston Symphony Orchestra (BSO). Boston, MA: Boston Symphony Orchestra, pp. 18–23.

Burlingame, J. (2015). Live Movie Concerts a Cash Cow for Orchestras. *Variety*, 29 April, https://variety.com/2015/music/features/live-movie-concerts-a-cash-cow-for-orchestras-1201483456.

Calabretto, R. (2010). *Lo schermo sonoro. La musica per film*. Venice: Marsilio.

Cariaga, D. (1984). Clearing the Air. *Los Angeles Times*, 3 August.

Christy, M. (1989). John Williams' Pursuit of Excellence. *Boston Globe*, 4 July.

Comuzio, E. (1980). *Colonna sonora. Dialoghi, musiche rumori dietro lo schermo*. Milan: Il Formichiere.

Cooke, M. (2008). *A History of Film Music*. Cambridge: Cambridge University Press.

Cooke, M., ed. (2010). *The Hollywood Film Music Reader*. New York: Oxford University Press.

Corbella, M. (2016). Il podio e lo schermo. La musica per film nella programmazione delle orchestre sinfoniche EIAR e RAI. In A. Malvano, ed., *La politica sinfonica della RAI: storia delle orchestre radio-televisive in Italia*. Alessandria: Edizioni dell'Orso, pp. 119–53.

Croce, B. (2005). *Estetica. Come scienza dell'espressione e linguistica generale*, 1902, ed. Giuseppe Galasso. Milan: Adelphi.

Dahlhaus, C. (1991). *The Idea of Absolute Music*, 1978, trans. Roger Lustig. Chicago/London: University of Chicago Press.

Dobroski, B. & Greene, C. (1984). Pass the Popcorn, An Interview with John Williams. *The Instrumentalist*, July, pp.6–9.

Downie Jr. , L. & Jolna, S. (1980). Boston Pops Goes Hollywood. *Washington Post*, 11 January.

Dyer, R. (1980a). John Williams is New Pops Maestro. A Musician's Musician. *Boston Globe*, 11 January.

Dyer, R. (1980b). Williams is Candidate for Fiedler's Job. *Boston Globe*, 6 January.

Dyer, R. (1980c). Mix Design and Mystery, You Get a Pops Maestro. *Boston Globe*, 10 January.

Dyer, R. (1980d). And a Good Concert, Too. *Boston Globe*, 30 April.

Dyer, R. (1980e). Q & A with John Williams. Pops Conductor Talks About His New Beat. *Boston Globe*, 27 April.

Dyer, R. (1980f). John Williams Bows In. *Boston Globe*, 11 January.

Dyer, R. (1981). Williams Poised for Pops. *Boston Globe*, 26 April.

Dyer, R. (1982). Orchestrating a New Pops Season. *Boston Globe*, 4 May.

Dyer, R. (1983). John Williams. Bringing Hollywood Magic to the Boston Pops. *Ovation*, June, pp. 12–15, 42–3.

Dyer, R. (1984). Williams, Pops in Harmony. *Boston Globe*, 19 August.

Dyer, R. (1985). Stars and Stripes Forever and Ever. *Boston Globe Sunday Magazine*, 28 April, pp. 10–14.

Dyer, R. (1988). Williams Says Pops Well-tempered for Upcoming Season. *Boston Globe*, 1 May.

Dyer, R. (1991a). Pops' Williams to Retire in '93. *Boston Globe*, 20 December.

Dyer, R. (1991b). Williams and the Art of the Pops. *Boston Globe*, 20 December.

Dyer, R. (1993). The Williams Years: Knowing What Counts. In concert booklet for 'Opening Night at Pops. A Gala Celebration for John Williams', 12 May 1993. Boston Symphony Archives, pp. 33–7.

Dyer, R. (1994). Williams to Stay on as Pops Adviser. *Boston Globe*, 4 February.

Dyer, R. (2002). Previn's Berlin Accent. *Boston Globe*, 10 March.

Ford, B. & Impemba, J. (1984). John Williams Quits Boston Pops. *Boston Herald*, 14 June.

Gilmore, P. S. (2010). *History of the National Peace Jubilee and Great Musical Festival: Held In the City of Boston*, 1871. Whitefish, MN: Kessinger.

Goodman, P. (1986). A Great Little Visiting Band. *New York Newsday*, 11 June.

Goodson, M. (1980). Yes, There's Life after Fiedler. *Boston Sunday Herald*, 27 January.

Gorbman, C. (1987). *Unheard Melodies. Narrative Film Music*. London/ Bloomington, IN: BFI/Indiana University Press.

Gordon, E. E. (1985). Research Studies in Audiation: I. *Bulletin of the Council for Research in Music Education* 84, 34–50.

Gorfinkle, C. (1984a). Williams Miffed by Hiss from Pops Orchestra? *Patriot Ledger*, 14 June.

Gorfinkle, C. (1984b). Why John Williams Changed His Mind. *Patriot Ledger*, 8 August.

Gorfinkle, C. (1984c). John Williams Now in Tune with His Players. *The Patriot Ledger*, 10 August.

Gorfinkle, C. (1985). 'Light Stuff' is Hard Work. *Patriot Ledger*, 15 January.

Hanslick, E. (1891). *The Beautiful in Music. A Contribution to the Revisal of Musical Aesthetics*, 1885, trans. Gustav Cohen. London: Novello.

Hasan, M. (2004). Musings of a Maestro. *Film Score Monthly*, October, pp.30–1.

Hinton, S. (2001). Gebrauchsmusik. *Grove Music Online*, www-oxfordmusiconline-com.proxy.lnu.se/grovemusic/view/10.1093/gmo/9781561592630.001.0001/omo-9781561592630-e-0000010804.

Humphrey, L. (1980). New Pops Era Recalls Another 50 Years Ago. *Boston Globe*, 1 May.

Irrgeher, C. (2020). John Williams: Sternstunden der Filmmusik. *Wiener Zeitung*, 20 January, www.wienerzeitung.at/nachrichten/kultur/klassik/2046653-John-Williams-Sternstunden-der-Filmmusik.html.

Jennes, G. (1980). The Boston Pops Gets a Movie Composer Who Doesn't Chase Fire Engines as Its New Boss. *People Weekly*, 23 June, pp. 47–52.

Karlin, F. (1994). *Listening to Movies. The Film Lover's Guide to Film Music*. Belmont, CA: Schirmer.

Karlin, F. & Wright, R. (2004). *On the Track. A Guide to Contemporary Film Scoring*, 2nd ed. New York/London: Routledge.

Kart, L. (1980). New Pops Chief Needs Time to Broaden Range. *Chicago Tribune*, 31 January.

Katz, L. (1984). Time for the Pops to Grow Up. *Boston Herald*, 1 July.

Katz, L. (1985). Dr. Hollywood & Mr. Pops. *Boston Herald*, 28 April.

Katz, L. (1989). John Williams and the Future of the Pops. *Boston Herald*, 5 May.

Kendall, L. (1992a). Music from Hollywood. *The Soundtrack Club*, April, p. 4.

Kendall, L. (1992b). 'Live' Cinema: Silents with Piano, Organ, Orchestral and Other Live Musical Accompaniment. *Film Score Monthly*, July, p. 6.

Kirshnit, F. (2006). New York Drops Off the List of 'Big Five' Orchestras. *New York Sun*, 5 December, www.nysun.com/arts/new-york-drops-off-the-list-of-big-five-orchestras/44570/.

Knight, M. (1980). John Williams Opens Season with Pops. *New York Times*, 30 April.

Lehman, F. (2018). Film-as-Concert Music and the Formal Implications of 'Cinematic Listening'. *Music Analysis* 37, 7–46.

Lehman, P. (2003). When Capitals Collide. Maestros Slatkin and Williams Join Forces for a Series of Film Music Festivities. *Film Score Monthly*, February 2003, pp. 12, 13, 47.

Levine, L. W. (1988). *Highbrow/Lowbrow: The Emergence of Cultural Hierarchy in America*. Cambridge, MA: Harvard University Press.

Livingstone, W. (1980). John Williams and the Boston Pops. An American Institution Enters a New Era. *Stereo Review*, December, pp.74–7.

Lockhart, K. (1996). Pops in Perspective. *Symphony Magazine*, November/December, pp. 27–32, 60–2.

Long, M. (2008). *Beautiful Monsters: Imagining the Classic in Musical Media*. Berkeley/Los Angeles, CA: University of California Press.

Lumsden, C. (1984). Pops Conductor, Angered by Hissing Exists Stage Left. *Gardner News*, 19 June.

Marmorstein, G. (1997). *Hollywood Rhapsody. Movie Music and Its Makers. 1900 to 1975*. New York: Schirmer.

Mazey, P. (2020). *British Film Music: Musical Traditions in British Cinema 1930s–1950s*. Basingstoke: Palgrave Macmillan.

McCorkle Okazaki, B. (2020). Liveness, Music, Media: The Case of the Cine-Concert. *Music and the Moving Image* 13(2), 3–24.

McKinnon, G. (1983). Williams Answers Spielberg's Call for Music. *Boston Globe*, 13 May.

McLellan, J. (1985). Pops Puts Emphasis on Masses. *Washington Post*, 18 July.

McLeod, K. (2006). 'A Fifth of Beethoven': Disco, Classical Music, and the Politics of Inclusion. *American Music* 24(3), 347–63.

Meyer, L. B. (1956). *Emotion and Meaning in Music*. Chicago/London: University of Chicago Press.

Meyer, L. B. (1967). *Music, the Arts, and Ideas. Patterns and Predictions in Twentieth-Century Culture*. Chicago/London: University of Chicago Press.

Meyer, L. B. (1996). *Style and Music. Theory, History, and Ideology*. Chicago/London: Chicago University Press.

Miceli, S. (1982). *La musica nel film. Arte e artigianato*. Fiesole: Discanto.

Miceli, S. (1999). Rai Radio 3 interview, 15 August 1999.

Miceli, S. (2009). *Musica per film. Storia, Estetica, Analisi, Tipologie*. Lucca/Milan: LIM/Ricordi.

Midgette, A. (2019). As a Classical Music Critic, I Used to Think the *Star Wars* Score Was Beneath Me. I Was Wrong. *Washington Post*, 18 January, www.washingtonpost.com/entertainment/music/as-a-classical-music-critic

-i-used-to-think-the-star-wars-score-was-beneath-me-i-was-wrong/2019/01/
17/80fe0744-18f0-11e9-88fe-f9f77a3bcb6c_story.html.

Miller, M. (1980). Williams: Two Pluses. *Boston Globe*, 10 January.

Miller, M. (1984a). Williams to Resign as Pops Conductor. *Boston Globe*, 14 June.

Miller, M. (1984b). The 'Tradition' that Cost Pops Its Conductor. *Boston Globe*, 15 June.

Montgomery, M. R. (1981). John Williams' Quiet Side. *Boston Globe*, 18 March.

Moss, P. (1984). A John Williams Triumph at Bowl. *Herald Examiner*, 15 September.

Neumeyer, D. & Platte, N. (2011). *Franz Waxman's Rebecca: A Film Score Guide*. Lanham, MD: Scarecrow.

Owades, S. H. (1980). Williams Good Choice at Helm of Pops. *Cincinnati Enquirer*, 15 February.

Page, T. (2003). Fade In: Soundtracks' Starring Role. *Washington Post*, 19 January, www.washingtonpost.com/archive/lifestyle/style/2003/01/19/fade-in-soundtracks-starring-role/808b7ff9-4dd8-4b7f-a4e3-135686915784/.

Paiste, D. (1993). Boston Pops Tradition Lives On. *New Hampshire Sunday News*, 9 May.

Pasles, C. (1988). John Williams Brings Bland Offerings to the Art Center. *Los Angeles Times*, 4 April.

Pearson, T. (2012). John Williams Interview with Classic FM. *ClassicFM.com*, 27 August, www.classicfm.com/music-news/pictures/composer/john-williams-interview-classic-fm/.

Pfeifer, E. (1980a). A Diary of the Pops Decision: How John Williams Got the Job. *Boston Herald American*, 13 January.

Pfeifer, E. (1980b). From Star Wars to Boston. *Boston Herald American*, 5 January.

Pfeifer, E. (1980c). A Legend Replaced with a Goldmine. *Boston Herald American*, 11 January.

Pfeifer, E. (1980d). Williams, 'I Never Intended to Conduct in Public'. *Boston Herald American*, 28 April.

Pfeifer, E. (1982). Play It Again, Maestro. John Williams Signs Up for a New Hitch. *Boston Herald*, 21 December.

Pfeifer, E. (1993). Passing the Baton. *Boston Sunday Herald*, 9 May.

Pfeifer, E. (1997). Williams Tinkers with Audio, Video. *Boston Herald*, 15 August.

Ponick, T. L. (2004). Movie Music Raised to Its Rightful Place by Composer. *Washington Times*, 3 December.

Reid, G. (2001). A Night of Surprises – Concerts In Review. *Film Score Monthly*, September, pp.9–10.

Rich, J. (2000). Evening at Pops: Putting on the Show. In *Boston Pops. The Story of America's Orchestra*. Boston Symphony Orchestra (BSO). Boston, MA: Boston Symphony Orchestra, pp. 44–7.

Rockwell, J. (1980). Traditionalist for the Pops. *New York Times*, 11 January.

Rosar, William H. (2003). Bernard Herrmann: The Beethoven of Film Music? *Journal of Film Music* 1(2–3), 121–50.

Ross, A. (2018). A Field Guide to the Musical Leitmotifs of *Star Wars*. *New Yorker*, 3 January, www.newyorker.com/culture/culture-desk/a-field-guide-to-the-musical-leitmotifs-of-star-wars.

Ross, A. (2020). The Force is Still Strong with John Williams. *New Yorker*, 21 July, www.newyorker.com/culture/persons-of-interest/the-force-is-still-strong-with-john-williams.

Rothemberg, F. (1983). Boston Pops Alters Concert Look in Wake of the Video Revolution. *Orlando Sentinel*, 16 July.

Safford, E. (1984). Pops Irritated Busy Williams. *Providence Journal*, 20 June.

Schneller, T. (2014). Sweet Fulfillment: Allusion and Teleological Genesis in John Williams's *Close Encounters of the Third Kind. The Musical Quarterly* 97(1), 98–131.

Score Masters: Celebrating John Williams and Jerry Goldsmith (2021). Podcast by the Ipswich Film Theatre, the Legacy of John Williams, the Goldsmith Odyssey, https://youtu.be/1bt3XCJG8gA.

Sloboda, J. (1999). *The Musical Mind. The Cognitive Psychology of Music*, new ed. Oxford/New York: Oxford University Press.

Smith, J. (1998). *The Sound of Commerce. Marketing Popular Film Music*. New York: Columbia University Press.

Smith, Steven C. (2002). *A Heart at Fire's Center: The Life and Music of Bernard Herrmann*, 2nd ed. Berkeley, CA: University of California Press.

Smith, Steven C. (2020). *Music by Max Steiner: The Epic Life of Hollywood's Most Influential Composer*. New York: Oxford University Press.

Smith, T. (2003). Maestro and the Movies. *Baltimore Sun*, 19 January.

Speyer, A. (1984). Pops Goes the Orchestra. *Berkshire Eagle*, 19 July.

Stearns, D. P. (1991). Hollywood Conductor Taps Studio Talent. *USA Today*, 31 July.

Stewart, R. H. (1984). We Didn't Drive Williams Away. *Boston Globe*, 8 July.

Sullivan, J. (2007). Conversations with John Williams. *The Chronicle of Higher Education*, 12 January, www.chronicle.com/article/ConversationsWithJohn/4906.

Swan, A., Kuflik, A., Donosky, L., & LaBrecque, R. (1980). Boston Pops Strikes Up the Band. *Newsweek*, 21 January, pp. 85–6.

Swed, M. (2012). Zubin Mehta's Heady Days as Los Angeles Philharmonic Music Director. *Los Angeles Times*, 8 December.

Wessel, D. (1983). The Force is with Him . . . 'Rich is Hard to Define'. *Boston Globe*, 5 July.

Wierzbicki, J. (2009). *Film Music: A History*. New York: Routledge.

Wierzbicki, J., Platte, N., & Roust, C., eds. (2012). *The Routledge Film Music Sourcebook*. New York: Routledge.

Winters, B. (2007a). Catching Dreams: Editing Film Scores for Publication. *Journal of the Royal Musical Association* 132(1), 115–40.

Winters, B. (2007b). *Erich Wolfgang Korngold's 'The Adventures of Robin Hood': A Film Score Guide*. Lanham, MD: Scarecrow.

Wood, D. B. (1985). Bang-Up Centennial at the Pops. *Christian Science Monitor*, 30 April.

Acknowledgements

This study is principally based on the research that I conducted in 2010 in the Boston Symphony Orchestra Archives and the WGBH Media Library and Archives. I was assisted by John Norris in the laborious perusal of decades of programme books and newspaper clippings, and with two sets of eyes we managed to process a decidedly superior amount of material.

In the following years, I augmented the findings with additional visits to the BSO Archives. My sincerest thanks for her assistance throughout the years go to BSO Archivist Bridget Carr, who also supervised the creation of 'Henry', BSO's performance history search engine, supported by grants from the National Endowment for the Humanities and the Alfred P. Sloan Foundation. Located at archives.bso.org, 'Henry' provides details for more than 32,000 performances given by the Boston Symphony Orchestra, the Boston Pops, the Boston Symphony Chamber Players, as well as the Tanglewood Music Center, including more than 27,000 concert programmes. The 'Henry' database has been an invaluable resource as I revisited my past findings in the preparation of this 'Element'.

Finally, I wish to express my gratitude to Mervyn Cooke for his most welcome invitation to contribute to the 'Music since 1945' Elements series from Cambridge University Press. My sincerest thanks also go to the anonymous reviewers that green-lit the publication and provided generous suggestions for improvement.

In loving memory of Bruno Cotti
(1921 – 2016)

Cambridge Elements ≡

Music since 1945

Mervyn Cooke
University of Nottingham

Mervyn Cooke brings to the role of series editor an unusually broad range of expertise, having published widely in the fields of twentieth-century opera, concert and theatre music, jazz, and film music. He has edited and co-edited *Cambridge Companions to Britten, Jazz, Twentieth-Century Opera*, and *Film Music*. His other books include *Britten: War Requiem, Britten and the Far East, A History of Film Music, The Hollywood Film Music Reader, Pat Metheny: The ECM Years*, and two illustrated histories of jazz. He is currently co-editing (with Christopher R. Wilson) *The Oxford Handbook of Shakespeare and Music*.

About the Series

Elements in Music since 1945 is a highly stimulating collection of authoritative online essays that reflects the latest research into a wide range of musical topics of international significance since the Second World War. Individual Elements are organised into constantly evolving clusters devoted to such topics as art music, jazz, music and image, stage and screen genres, music and media, music and place, immersive music, music and movement, music and politics, music and conflict, and music and society. The latest research questions in theory, criticism, musicology, composition and performance are also given cutting-edge and thought-provoking coverage. The digital-first format allows authors to respond rapidly to new research trends, with contributions being updated to reflect the latest thinking in their fields, and the essays are enhanced by the provision of an exciting range of online resources.

Cambridge Elements≡

Music since 1945

Elements in the Series